THE
ASKING
LEADER

MIKE LOGAN

First published in 2019 by Mike Logan

The moral rights of the author have been asserted.

Editing + Proofreading by Cavalletti Communications, www.cavacom.biz
Cover Design by Melanie Allen (www.keo.com.au)
Typesetting by Self-Publishing Lab

Disclaimer
The material in this publication is of the nature of general comment only, and does not represent professional advice. It is not intended to provide specific guidance for particular circumstances and it should not be relied on as the basis for any decision to take action or not take action on any matter which it covers. Readers should obtain professional advice where appropriate, before making any such decision.

To the maximum extent permitted by law, the author and publisher disclaim all responsibility and liability to any person, arising directly or indirectly from any person taking or not taking action based on the information in this publication.

ISBN 978-0-646-80333-3 (pbk)

Contents

Dedication

Firstly, I would like to dedicate this book to my staff. Those poor people who suffered through my learning. They saw me through some awkward decisions with grace, patience and good humour.

Secondly, my CEOs. Those wonderful business leaders who have developed the Asking Leader with me. They have seen me develop the idea as I have sat with them in their offices and meeting rooms. Many times, they have seen me stain my clothes with whiteboard markers as I have learnt with them.

Finally, my fellow directors. I have sat on many boards with great people who were usually older and always wiser. I have been guided by master Chairmen to understand the practice and subtlety of guiding their boards to good decisions. If I can mention one, it is George Davey AM. A gentleman and a master persuader.

What a privilege!

Acknowledgements

My editors Daniela Cavalletti and Jessica Stewart. They have guided me into my first book with style and skill.

Always, my family. Terry and my two (adult) children Henry and Isabel.

There is one key person that saw in me the capacity to reinvent myself from crusty old farmer to business mentor. Stephanie Christopher, CEO of The Executive Connection.

Finally, two old blokes who are no longer with us. These old fellas were my first mentors and I am forever grateful to them for the calm guidance in the face of my frenetic ambition. They are Bruce Mackey and Ian Hamparsum. They were true gentlemen of the bush.

Prologue

It's funny, this getting old.

People are quite forgiving. They forgive my funny old habits, silly dad jokes, forgetting their names, mangling my syntax and heaven only knows any personal habits they politely don't mention.

Relationships are different too. I have found tolerance and patience. I have found the love of my life. Those things are probably interconnected.

Professionally, I have made a metamorphic change to my role. For thirty years I was a farmer and now I am not. Moving away from a life's work was not an easy decision. I had imagined that creating a new life and role in society was going to be difficult.

It wasn't.

It has been wonderful fun to learn and grow into a new role at my age. It still is.

This book started as a journal of that journey. Every time I learnt something that made me grow in my role, I would write it down. Then it occurred to me that all the speakers, trainers, books, seminars, podcasts and TED talks were telling me to ask questions.

But no one was telling me how. How to ask questions.

All my studies taught me what would happen if I did ask questions – success, change, engagement, time to think, more holidays and more.

In a word: leadership.

If I could learn to ask questions, good questions, well-structured questions and listen properly to the answers, I would be a leader.

The Asking Leader.

My initial reaction was that the idea was too simple. Too obvious. So, I tested it with my clients.

I was half-right: it is simple and effective. But it is hard. It is difficult to maintain the self-discipline to be the Asking Leader. It is so hard that I, too, struggle with the self-discipline to remain in the mode of the Asking Leader.

But when I do, I lead. When my clients do, they successfully achieve their goals, introduce and manage change, have an engaged, motivated & accountable workplace and give themselves time to work on the higher-order aspects of their businesses.

And they go on more holidays.

Can you be the Asking Leader?

Introduction to the Asking Leader

When I became a CEO it was not because anyone appointed me. I just became CEO of my own business. I grew my business so that I needed a CEO and I was damned if it wasn't going to be me. By my mid twenties, I was in full flight as a CEO, full of energy, ambition and not a little bravery.

I was content rich and process free. I was insufficiently curious and totally without discipline. Just hard work and guts.

I now think that I was the same as 99.9 per cent of all CEOs who are starting in business.

To counter all my energy, I was hindered by a complete lack of wisdom. Completely without insight.

Go on, tell me that wasn't (or isn't) you too.

I had taken over the smouldering remnants of one of the old family businesses that began in the early 1950s. I was just married and I sat in a meeting with the bank and asked for a break. I would recover the business in five years or they could close me down. My new wife thought she had married a wealthy farmer. We were broke.

The bank had few options. Sell me up and take a whopping loss or hope I could recover something. They chose hope. I can only imagine the bullshit story they told their credit committee.

To give the bank their credit, five years later they wrote me a letter and said, 'Repay the loan.' Circumstances and hard yakka had worked for me and I was able to go to another bank and refinance. I had built a business that had a reasonably strong cash flow, but a very poor asset base. I found a (then) young banker who bought the story of cash flow to service the debt. He went with me and I repaid his support. We're still mates.

It took 25 years to fully pay off the loan. That's farming.

My role as a CEO grew. I became sufficiently curious to go and find out what I should be doing. I joined the Australian Institute of Management (AIM) and did many of their short courses, did a company directors course with the Australian Institute of Company Directors (AICD) and every other course they offered, went through the first intake of the Australian Rural Leadership Program and employed the best consultants I could find and afford.

Like many of my peers, I've always struggled to have the discipline to properly implement the processes I knew were needed.

Now I have that wisdom. Earnt through experience and commitment to learning.

My grandfather was a typical character of the bush. Jovial and a bit cunning. He used to say that, 'if you put two people into a room—one has the money and one has the experience—at the end of the meeting, the one with the money will have an experience, and the one with the experience will walk out with the money'. I can now walk out with some money.

This book is about me continuing to learn. It is my quest to become the Asking Leader. Come with me and see what we can learn together.

Why develop the idea of the Asking Leader?

My recent life has been in the field of coaching CEOs through The Executive Connection (TEC). I run a group of CEOs who range in age and business skills. Although the training we receive as new Chairmen at TEC is excellent, there was something missing in the training.

CEOs want to start with the decision: they have no time to find out more, ask deeper questions and develop a shared solution. CEOs think, 'Give me the problem and I will solve it. Now'.

It is usually their decision and often it is final. No one else owns it, there is often insufficient consultation and if it fails … the poor old CEO is a loner. The only way that CEO is going to have any friends is to buy a dog.

I have spent the past several years trying to unpack the notion of being a CEO coach. I have searched for a simple and memorable rule that I can apply in every situation.

Initially, my methodology was to listen to all the guest presenters and trainers we bring to our groups and remind the members of the group of our learnings. It was then that it struck me that all I was doing was teaching my members to ask questions.

In fact, it is to Ask a Series of Questions – or ASQ.

The idea is too simple to survive any rational examination or peer review. But what works?

I quickly came up with a simple methodology that I can apply in nearly every circumstance and more importantly, I can remember it! At my age, that is important!

An even better way to remember the idea and learn to apply it, was to write it down. Thus, this book. This book is to teach myself.

You are collateral damage. You can learn with me.

Soon enough it occurred to me that the best thing I could do is to teach my CEOs the idea. I booked myself as my own guest speaker for that month and gave the presentation as if I was giving it to any group of CEOs.

It worked. The idea is now a mantra in the group: 'What are the questions we need to ask to resolve this issue?'

That is how I decided to become the Asking Leader. My goal is to teach CEOs to ASQ so they will grow. Grow their businesses, themselves, their employees and their relationships.

I decided this was even better than buying a dog.

To let us learn together, let's engage with each other. Actually, can you continue to teach me? Can we pick up these basic leadership principles that you will learn through the book and improve them? If you agree that the Asking Leader is just a starting point to adapt our leadership style then, together, can we continually improve on these basic principles?

If we can continually improve the idea, could that improve our own leadership behaviours? Can that change in our behaviour materially change the performance of our businesses, our people and our own lives?

Can we measure those changes that come from our own change to becoming the Asking Leader?

If we can agree to work together on this, how could we do that? What are the ways we could work together to continually improve on the Asking Leader?

Throughout the book you will see references to the website, www. askingleader.com. There will be a series of pages there where you can contribute to the conversation. In each circumstance of your Asking Leader journey, as you change your leadership behaviours, write in and tell us what worked well, what could have been better and what new ideas or series of questions you will use.

There are no wrong answers here. There are no stupid ideas. Let's try each series of questions and analyse why they worked … or didn't.

Are you the manager who has the answers?
Or
The leader who asks the questions?

The transition from manager to leader is dependent on one critical factor: asking.

If you can move from being the manager with the answers to the leader who asks the right questions you will:

- have more time to be effective
- make more money
- be recognised as a business leader, a good person, a smart person, caring and fair
- build capacity in your people to run your business
- learn and grow, be open to ideas
- have an open mind, be courageous and humble
- have strong opinions while being open to new perspectives.

If you want it enough, this book will show you how to be that person.

Are you the leader who asks the right questions?

Can you ask questions? Can you create the mindset to become the Asking Leader?

Do you have the **self-discipline** to ask more than one question? Do you have the self-discipline to plan the next conversation by designing a *series of questions*?

Can you **listen**? Can you listen properly with all your senses? Can you hold the self-discipline to be completely **curious**?

Do you have the self-discipline to use the questions to create accountability? Can you ask a series of questions that achieves the **accountability** that your business needs?

Finally, are you capable of **changing yourself** to become the leader that you aspire to be? Are you sufficiently motivated to change the way you behave as a CEO to achieve this standard of leadership?

OR, are you the business manager with all the answers?

Do your people come to you with every problem? Is it hard to find the right people? Do your people even like working in your business?

Do you have time to work **on** your business? Do you have enough time to consider your strategy? Have you considered the purpose of the business? Can your business grow? Are you the limitation to the business growth?

Is your business dependent on you being there? Can you take holidays with confidence? Do you feel that your people are accountable for their responsibilities?

Which do you want to be? The leader who asks, or the manager who answers?

Ask yourself:

- how much do you want to be that type of leader?
- how much do you want to change yourself to become that leader?

- which of the aspects listed here are the biggest motivator for you?
- which are the biggest challenges for you?
- why are they challenging?

If you do want to change yourself .... let's cinch up and go on the journey to become the Asking Leader.

Part 1:

What is the Asking Leader? How it works

What is the Asking Leader?

The Asking Leader has the self-discipline to design and ask a series of questions to learn and to grow their business. Designing and asking a series of questions will create engagement and accountability.

The first challenge for CEOs (myself as much as anyone!) is to:

Listen like a leader

Not

Speak like a dictator.

Did you know that LISTEN is an anagram for SILENT?

We all find it easy to dictate our decisions and we find it tedious to consult. We naturally err to the statement rather than having the discipline to ask the questions. Then, when we do ask the questions, we are usually listening for what we want to hear. We have an in-built filter that comes from the desire to control.

That is why we are CEOs. It is exactly the driven personality type that got us into the CEOs big leather chair.

Asking Leader is the other way. The Asking Leader **ends** with the decision.

We must have the discipline to manage our need to control. We must learn to listen properly. Like Socrates who knows nothing (and he is not even sure about that). We must learn to mine the contribution from our staff and expect to find gold in there.

Asking Leader is a simple guideline that all CEOs can use in all circumstances. No matter the decision to be made, or the guidance needed by the CEO, Asking Leader will get them to the best decision with their dignity intact – and no need for a dog.

It is never just one killer question that the CEO should ask. The Asking Leader knows to design and ask a series of questions to get the successful result.

It follows a simple principle:

Tell me and I will **listen**
Show me and I will **see**
Ask me and I will **understand**
Become an Asking Leader and we will **learn and grow.**

We will grow our:

- business
- profits
- margins
- sales
- employee retention
- employee attraction
- relationships
- professional capacity
- future.

We will grow our Senior Leadership Teams' (SLT) capacity to lead their own teams. Most importantly, we will grow ourselves as leaders.

Think about it on two planes. It is often said that leadership is a magic blend of **discipline and curiosity**.

It is the **discipline** to design and ask a series of questions and the **curiosity** to listen to the answers.

So, let's break them down to find the genesis of the two concepts:

1. Curiosity

Curiosity goes back to Socrates. Poor old Socrates asked so many questions that he became annoying. He was the original cool cat killed by his curiosity. He was so annoying the Greek government of the day had him executed in 399BC – how did the Greeks know to count backwards to the birth of Jesus 399 years later?

The trial of Socrates was quite a democratic process where he had been charged with 'failing to acknowledge the gods that the city acknowledges' and 'introducing new deities.' He was executed by drinking the poisonous beverage of hemlock. It must have been an awful death. Hemlock causes the respiratory muscles to paralyse and choke the heart and brain of oxygen. You wouldn't wish that on your worst enemy.

The simplest statement on curiosity from Socrates is:

"I only know one thing; that I know nothing. I am not even sure about that."

He tried to keep his mind completely open so that he could absorb more knowledge. In so doing, his life's work was about how to absorb more knowledge. He wanted to teach people concepts that became scepticism, critical thinking, pedagogy and cross-examination.

These days people think of scepticism as incredulity. It is that they don't believe. It is now about denial more than inquiry. The original Greek word for sceptic was 'sképtomai' which means 'to inquire'. To inquire, you must have curiosity.

Socrates never actually wrote anything. All of his teachings were interpreted by Plato in his Socratic dialogue entitled, *'The Republic'* (380BC). Scholars for more than 2,400 years have thought about the lessons of Socrates. For my purposes, I use the Six Types of Socratic Questions (you know you have arrived when they turn your name into an adjective). I rely heavily on the need to:

1. understand the issue more deeply
2. probe the assumptions that are usually inherent
3. probe for evidence
4. challenge the viewpoints and perspectives
5. discover the implications and consequences
6. go back to the beginning and understand if that was really the question.

Often, the simplest and most effective question
is only one word: 'Why?'

In this century, we can refer to Simon Sinek and Ricardo Semler. Simon Sinek[1] said it so simply:

'Start with Why.'

Ricardo Semler[2] said nearly the same thing sixteen years earlier.

'Ask 3 'whys' in a row.'

The great leaders have curiosity. They have the innate capacity to inquire with an open mind so they can learn and grow. Great leaders give the impression that they only know the question – and not the answer.

"I have no special talents. I am only passionately curious."
Albert Einstein

2. Discipline (actually, self-discipline)

Lots of people will confuse 'discipline' with 'imposed discipline'. In this context, we are talking about self-discipline. It is about having the discipline to control both the situation and yourself to get the most productive outcome.

Some may call it emotional intelligence. That is, having the self-discipline and control to calmly and logically be fully curious.

---

1   Simon Sinek, *Start with Why*, Portfolio, New York, 2009
2   Ricardo Semler, *Maverick*, Warner Books, New York, 1993

Simply, it is having the self-discipline to be patient. Do you have the self-discipline to stop yourself going immediately to the decision? In this instance, the best route to great decisions is not the shortest.

Ask yourself:

How do you put your emotions aside to be fully curious?
How do you manage yourself to be patient and thorough?

This self-discipline is not about obeying the rules of others; it is about obeying your own rules.

So how can we be properly curious? How can we have the discipline to encourage and allow our people, our team members, employees and customers the privilege of their contribution? How can we be sufficiently patient and polite to allow our stakeholders their input?

The front row forward from the Australian Rugby team, the *Wallabies*, Ben Darwin said:

'When in doubt, the answer is usually in the room.'

And we could adapt what Steve Jobs said so simply:

"It doesn't make sense to hire smart people and tell them what to do; we hire smart people and ask them what we should do."

Asking Questions—
the long road

I love this cartoon by Wiley's Non Sequitur series! The left turn over the cliff is where everyone is going. However, the right turn off into the future has a little bookshelf on it. The road is long and has many bends. There are very few people on it. You must read some books and do some homework.

The manager with all the answers may be going over that cliff. The Asking Leader is on the long road. Let's get on that road.

Do you know the time when you are struck down by the need to make a decision? It could be a decision that you need to make now, or one that you need to make over time.

Your brain freezes and you go directly to the decision. You forget that:

- there are other people who may want to have input
- there are more aspects to the problem than even your brilliant mind can compute
- there may be drastic unintended consequences of the wrong decision.

'We will do this …' If this is the way you are going to manage people, buy a dog. It's the only way you will have any friends. I recommend a Labrador. They are faithful, forgiving and don't really want to give their point of view. They are bigger than a Jack Russell, but the only time you should call a Jack Russell is when it is already coming towards you. The Jack Russell is not a good listener and will not be a good companion of the manager who already has all the answers.

Why ask questions – rather than just give the answers in the time-honoured manner of the business manager? What does the method of asking questions create that dictating doesn't?

The business leader usually wants two things: ownership and accountability. Asking questions achieves both and dictating achieves neither.

The manager with the answers will dictate the strategy or the solution to the problem at hand and the faithful team member will go and execute it as well as possible. If it doesn't work, it is the manager's fault. When it comes time to measure the success of the solution, the team member says, 'I tried my best but your solution didn't work'. There is no ownership and no accountability.

The Asking Leader with the questions will ask how the problem can be solved. Then the Asking Leader will ask when it will be done and how will we know it has been achieved. The team member will have ownership of the solution and be accountable for it.

Do a little test in your organisation. Watch people react when you solve the problem for them by giving them the solution. How much do they own the solution and how accountable are they for it?

Then, turn it around. Watch how they react when you ask them to recommend a solution. Did they react differently?

This is the fundamental shift in your mindset. The shift is how you as the CEO react to daily challenges of your role. You will find that asking them to find their own solutions will create deeper ownership in the outcome. They will sign on to their own ideas with more vigour.

If your mindset can shift, can you then ask them to shift their mindsets to train their own teams to own the solutions?

Not all questions are created equal

Do you know what type of question you are asking? How you ask each question has an impact on the quality of the answer you receive. We must **demonstrate** to our staff, customers, shareholders and families that we value their views.

In simple terms there are, for our purposes, four types of questions:

1. closed questions: is this a closed question – yes/no
2. solution-oriented questions: questions that have the answer woven into them
3. one killer question: we need to have the discipline to accept that there is not one question but a series of questions

4. rambler questions: we need to be concise in our questions so that we
    don't offer three or four different nuances to the one simpler question.

1. Closed Questions.

Here's a trick. To stop yourself (self-discipline) asking **closed
questions,** you will need to train yourself to ask open questions. It is
this simple.

Reframe the question:

from:

> Do you have any other options?
> Could there be other ways?
> Is there a way?
> Can you do that?

to:

> What could you do?
> How would you?
> How else could we?
> What other options?

It's this simple. As Rudyard Kipling said in his poem *Elephant's Child,*

> "I keep six honest serving-men
> (They taught me all I knew);
> Their names are What and Why and When
> And How and Where and Who."
> **Rudyard Kipling**

The important line in that excerpt is the second one: "They taught me all I knew". Elegantly, he makes the link between curiosity and learning.

2. Solution-Oriented Questions

Can you resist the urge to ask **Solution-Oriented Questions**? It takes self-discipline.

A solution-oriented question comes all neatly packaged with an answer attached. It is usually the answer you have already intuitively concluded.

Rather than: 'Shouldn't you check in with your head of digital before you make this decision?'

You could ask: 'Who else should you consult as you make this decision?'

Rather than: 'Do you think you should ask your sales manager about this first?'

You could ask: 'Is there any more research you think you need? Who could you ask?'

3. The Rambler Question

The **Rambler Question** is when the CEO is phrasing a question and simultaneously thinking out aloud. If the question was 'what do you want to do'?, then you are tempted to fill out that question with some thoughts of your own. These thoughts are not solutions, just discussion points that are rolling around in your head as you speak.

The extrovert CEOs are often prone to rambling. They just like the sound of their own voice and they think aloud, with their mouths wide open and flapping like a mainsail on a yacht that is head-to-wind.

When the team member pauses, they will fill the silence with their own noise. They can't stand the silence and aren't sufficiently patient to let their team member think and consider a response.

By confusing the question with too much contextual background and white noise, the team member gets distracted from the original purpose of the discussion. The impact is that conversation will often bear off course. It is then up to the team member to bring the CEO back to the subject they were discussing.

4. The Killer Question

Once CEOs start asking questions, they want to do it in one step. This is called the **'killer question'.** Many CEOs fall into this trap.

'If you've got a problem, what are you going to do about it?' is a killer question. The CEO feels all-powerful and the team member feels belittled. There has been no discussion about:

- the problem itself
- any impacts of the problem
- what would happen if the problem was solved
- possible solutions.

The killer question did not allow any ownership and only insisted on the accountability.

Is the so-called 'Killer Question' effective?

My client runs a great business. He is flying. Profitable, growing, retaining customers and expanding into new markets overseas. His issue for resolution was his marketing manager. He decided to cut costs and reduce the marketing spend while they were heavily booked delivering product already sold. His marketing manager had worked hard to develop relationships with trade magazines, websites and social media platforms. The cutback meant that the work she had done felt as though it had been wasted. She wasn't feeling valued in the company and wanted a broader role as the company grew out of its need for marketing spending. He said to her, 'What do you want to do?'

He had asked the killer question.

Her answer was curt, 'I don't know!'

I asked him how he could have rephrased the question into a series of questions. If the ultimate question was 'What do you want to do?' then the preceding questions could have introduced the idea without as much confrontation.

We decided it could have been:

'What do you like about your current role? What don't you like?'

'What tasks and challenges do you do first? Which do you put off to last?'

'Which gaps do you see in our structure that need filling? How would they align with your strengths and interests?'

Ultimately, my client decided to do a DISC (Dominance, Influence, Steadiness, Conscientiousness) profile on his marketing manager so that they could assess her strengths, interests, inclinations, and preferences – she's still with the company.

Owning the solutions

When I first became a TEC Chairman, I was thrust into one-to-one interviews with each of our members, without any training. I was given a form entitled, *Great One-to-One Questions*.

To me the questions sounded like something from one of those personal coaching sessions where the client is asked:

- 'What is keeping you up at night?'
- 'What topic are you hoping I don't bring up?'
- 'If you were competing with your company, what would you do?'
- 'What is the most important thing we should be talking about today?'

They are all good questions, but I still had the feeling that they were cheap. It took me a long time to work it out.

They were 'one killer questions'. There was no series of questions to dig deeper.

Those questions encouraged me to go to the solutions.

- 'If that is keeping you up at night, what are you going to do about it?'

Too soon, I was making my own suggestions. I was moving from coach to mentor. With my younger clients, I was even more inclined to become their mentor. They would look at me and agree. 'Yes, I will do that.' 'You are right, I need to do that.'

I was building the solutions and they didn't own them. Next month I would come back, and it wasn't done. My clients may have agreed on the solution, but they didn't own it.

 It may have been the right solution, but it wasn't theirs.

It was the same when I was a business owner. My farm managers would come in to see me with a problem and I would solve it. Right there and then. 'Do this ...'

My best farm manager, Steve, would actually get upset that I didn't explore the issue a bit more with him. He would say that I have solved the issue, but that wasn't necessarily what he wanted. It took me too long to work out that what he wanted was to talk about it a bit more. He wanted to think about it, roll it around in our minds until we understood it more deeply, then work out ways to solve it.

Eventually, I saw his point.

I didn't know how to have that conversation at the beginning. I did not have the tools in my mind. I did not have the curiosity or the discipline to build a process that would create a decision that he owned.

There were four things I didn't have right:

- I didn't know **how** to have that conversation. I did not have the tools in my mind. I did not have the curiosity or the discipline to build a process that would create a decision that he owned.
- I didn't have the **humility** to acknowledge that my managers may have had a better solution than me.
- I didn't have the **patience** to wait for the answers or work my way into finding the right answers.
- I didn't understand that by asking deeper and deeper questions, people are more likely to **find their own advice**. It surprised me to learn that they are far more likely to take their own advice than mine.

I needed to be the Asking Leader and quietly ASQ with a WISPA.

Rating: How good are you?

- If you had to give yourself a rating out of 10 for asking, where would you rate yourself? Do you:
  - Know how to ask open questions?
  - Have the humility to accept the ideas of your team?
  - Commit the time and have the patience to work towards the best answers?
  - Understand the power of letting your team find their own advice and accountability?

- If you got someone else to ask your Senior Leadership Team, Board, shareholders, key clients the same question, how would they rate you out of 10?
- Where would you like to be rated out of 10?
- What can you do about achieving that desired rating?
- What are you going to do?
- How will we know you have changed?

A Series of Questions

Now that you have framed the issues in a question—some questions—a CEO needs to have the discipline to stand back from the issue at hand (often fraught and intense – emotional) and work out a way to solve the issue.

A way to solve the issue is in a *series of questions*.

A series of questions is the antidote to the one killer question. This is the principle at the very heart of the Asking Leader concept. The Asking Leader must allow the time to get deeper into every issue so that they create the ownership and accountability that will drive the business forward.

The series of questions is not the solution to the issue; it is the pathway to the decision. The Asking Leader has the discipline to thoroughly follow the series. The Asking Leader knows that the series is always more than a question and an answer. It is much more sophisticated than one question. It is the discipline to *ask a **series** of questions* that achieves an answer.

Let's ask a killer question:

CEO: 'Do you think this is a good idea?'
Employee: 'Er, yes boss.'
CEO: 'Good. Let's do it then. Report back in a week.'

As my daughter would say;

'Epic fail Dad.'

Or, we can Ask A Series of Questions. More than Ask, we can ASQ.

Stop doing and start thinking: a personal story

There are many remote places on this earth and the Kimberley in north-west Western Australia is one of them. It is a landscape of enormous proportions and vibrant colours of bright orange rocks and soil, the occasional splash of green boab trees, very little water, and mostly dry, brown spinifex grass. Wherever you turn it is endless and without empathy. It is one of those uncomfortable places you go to so that you can say that you have been there. Once you are there, you will be charmed by it.

The Kimberley landscape cannot simply be described as rugged. It is ancient, worn by so much time, weary of the millennia. There is no symmetry in the Kimberley. There are no straight lines, rounded shapes or simple colours – except for the perfect, blue daytime sky.

The Kimberley is about time. Being there makes you recognise the passing of the millions of years our little speck in the universe has orbited around our sun. You find yourself looking at the landscape and appreciating the time through which it has survived. When you are there, you wonder why? It is beautiful, but you wonder. It is like climbing Everest so that you can say you had. I went to the Kimberley many times and I can say that I have.

To have lived in this environment as the Aborigines have done is testimony to their resilience. Those souls who achieve breeding age and parenthood in this vast, dry landscape are beyond anyone's imagination of endurance.

The people we meet along the way are a product of the environment. Their skin is dry and wrinkled, their clothes have absorbed the dust so that the colours merge, their hat is never new – even if it is bought a month ago. Their voices sound of the dry wind and their words are close to an unintelligible mumble with lips that barely move to prevent the unwelcome intrusion of the flies. Their boots were often non-existent. Sometimes they wore rubber thongs and sometimes ventilated Blundstones. Rarely did I see any socks.

That their cars actually took them anywhere was a wonder of modern engineering. In a place where a reliable vehicle could mean the difference between life and death, they choose to drive wrecks held together with the ingenuity of the bush people and the charity of whatever has been left lying beside the road.

This trip was my first. I was in a group of young agricultural people who all aspired to be leaders – not the least of which was me. The group was tasked to travel across this vast, rugged and unforgiving landscape for ten days. There were various activities along the way to distract us from the hunger, heat, cold, thirst, and pain. We had to climb cliffs, navigate caves of limestone and large lizards, build a boat out of whatever we could find to cross a crocodile-infested river. The exercise was about survival in a group.

There was not a lot of support except for our own internal resources and a facilitator who, in my group of six, was Paul. I thought Paul was mute. Paul was quiet. Very pleasant but said very little. It was difficult to learn much about him, but we prised from him that he was a mining engineer from Mount Isa.

Paul would quietly trudge along with our group with his remarkably lightly loaded backpack. We trudged along with our overloaded backpacks and thought about how much we actually needed to have carried in this far corner of our earth.

After six or seven days our personal hygiene had progressed beyond the stage where we noticed our own odour. The fine red dust, spiked spinifex scratching our knees with every step and the personal grime of many miles walking in the heat all made for a particular bush smell that we no longer noticed.

We were traversing a particularly stark landscape one night. We were not only quite lost and without any form of communication, we had been given the wrong maps. We learnt later this was intentional. It was one of the insidious tricks played upon us by our ex-military convenors. Doubtless, these scheming bastards thought the trick to be amusing.

The night sky makes you notice that our place in this vast universe is infinitesimal. In the Kimberley, the night sky is unusually vast. I could see up into the stars and see not space, but time. The light from those stars left them thousands of years ago and arrived in the Kimberley on that night.

I am used to the night sky so visible in the bush – away from the city lights and accompanying pollution. As a farmer I have always been an irrigator. I have often been up at night, changing the syphons, balancing the water supply and flow with the consumption by my crop. I would often pause from my water and crop to look into the magic of the night sky. My wide, flat and featureless farm was always lost in the night sky. I would pick out the Southern Cross and the Pointers to find due south. I would trace the Milky Way across the sky to meet the Saucepan. I would track it across the sky each night.

The Kimberley sky is different. Different stars, bigger again. I have always felt small at night in the bush; in the Kimberley I was smaller again. The vastness always makes me feel alone but never vulnerable. The night sky gives me a feeling of joy. The more urban, indoor types in our group were in the early stages of agoraphobia. The night sky gave them no joy. No hope. The circumstances developed an understandable anxiety.

I am an experienced aeroplane pilot and of the view that I can competently read a map. I approached the map with the overconfidence that proved our downfall. In the dark of that night, I successfully made the wrong map fit the landscape we were in. I made the darkened valleys, dry creeks and mountains appear on our map as if by magic. We continued to get more lost, tired, hungry, and frustrated.

We were beginning to get desperate and were not far from a full-scale panic. We were past the point where we could accept any discussion about emotional intelligence. We were not yet at the life or death stage. We were not yet looking at the fat people in the group and wondering if we would have to eat them.

We asked Paul what we should do. Our apparently mute facilitator looked at me for a while. Silently and without a glimmer of expression. His answer has stuck with me all these years. He said:

"That is a content question; I will only answer a process question."

Our response to this statement was in an order of emotions. Initially we looked at him blankly. We then realised he was not going to help. We saw ourselves through a murderous phase. We lowered down to the 'grievous bodily harm' phase for a few moments. Finally, with eyes red of frustration and dust, we calmed down sufficiently to ask the next question:

"What is the difference between content and process?"

The actual question we asked was burdened with many unprintable expletives.

It was then that I learnt that process is being able to ask a series of questions that will resolve the issue. The content is the discussion that revolves around the issue itself. The decision came from the discussion that had been guided by the series of questions we had asked ourselves.

That is what this book is about. How do we have the discipline to train ourselves to ask a series of questions that will resolve our issues, problems, strategies, or whatever? How can we be sufficiently curious to fully understand each decision?

With the series of questions in mind, we could now look at the content of the issues of the moment to create great decisions. In the darkness of the Kimberley night, tired, hungry, thirsty, and lost, this was a difficult lesson to learn. But learn it we must if we wanted advice from our expressionless Paul.

He didn't give us any advice. He just asked us what is the issue we are trying to resolve and how were we going to resolve it together? To state the bleeding obvious, the issue was to get safe and find our destination. But his continued question back to us was: 'How were we going to resolve the issue of getting safe and finding our destination?'

The question wasn't, 'How do we get safe and find the destination?' but 'How do we decide how to get safe and find our destination? What process will we follow to survive?' Today, I know we had to be the Asking Leader. What process should we use? What series of questions should we ask ourselves? We had to stop going forward, creating activity, soldiering on. We had to stop 'doing' and start 'thinking'.

We were six blokes and one woman. The blokes wanted to 'do'. The woman in our group had spent the day explaining to us the beauty of the colours of the Kimberley. Wonderful ochres of the rocks, the golden crown of the spinifex. She was the only one happy to stop and think. We thought Kate was a pain in the arse.

Kate was the only one who was right.

Exhausted, with urgent needs, we had to pause and work out what was the series of questions we needed to ask ourselves before we could finally make some progress.

Only then we could go forward.

We worked out what our needs were, what our resources were (including that the map was a method to distract us by the evil plotters who organised the course), what was important and what wasn't. We stepped above our situation to resolve the issue together.

From a content perspective, we could see the highway off in the distance as the occasional road train went by. From the top of a hill we could see the glimmer of lights of what we thought was the township of Fitzroy Crossing. We estimated it to be 40 kms or more away. We took a bearing from there and worked out a line on a map where we could be. We then took some shots from the distant highway and tried to work out where those two lines transected. That gave us a rough position. Then we worked out how far we were from where we needed to go. Then worked out what was between those two points. We decided to sleep where we were because time was not the critical factor that we had imagined. We were so tired.

Needless to say, we all lived. The next morning, at first light, the world became clearer. We got to our objective late that afternoon.

Along the way, in our exhaustion and discomfort, we worked out that we needed to pause and work out a series of questions to ask ourselves before we could go forward – and survive.

This works anywhere. Stop doing and start thinking. Before 'We will do this,' you will need to train yourself to pause. Breathe. Then WISPA quietly to yourself. You will need to train yourself to design a series of questions that will meet the needs of the decision.

So, what is WISPA?

Some decisions will have particular aspects that will require you to design a targeted series of questions. They may be in marketing, HR, production and so on. However, most decisions have five key aspects: the WISPA aspects: 'What' is the issue, the 'Impacts', measuring 'Success', deciding on a Plan, and defining 'Accountabilities'.

1. **W**hat is the issue?

What is the background to this issue? Define the problem, the challenge, the central question. Discuss the background to the issue.

This seems pretty simple, but it is amazing how often we rush from issue to solution. This rule is to slow down the rush to solution. The first step is to **get agreement** on the actual issue.

Symptom or cause? Often, we solve the wrong problem by focussing on the symptom of the problem rather than the deeper cause. We have to commit time and discipline to being curious about the real issue. Discovery of the deeper cause is often the break that only excellent leaders can find.

Ownership – often, we are solving issues with hasty solutions that people don't yet *own*. The people whom we, as leaders, are trying to influence have not been properly heard. The challenge is having the discipline to be patient while continuing to be curious. Hugh Mackay says that, "people are more likely to support a change if they are consulted before the change is made".[3]

1.1 Why do you think this issue is important?

1.2 What is the background of the issue? Where did it come from?

---

3 Hugh Mackay, *Why don't people listen?*, Macmillan Australia, 2013

2. **What are the Impacts of the issue?**

   Look at the financial, emotional, time and team impacts.

   Now that we have talked about it:

   2.1   What do we now think of the issue?

   2.2   Is it actually the problem or have we identified something else?

   2.3   What is the issue now? Restate the issue.

3. **What does Success look like?**

   If we were to solve the problem what would the solution achieve?

 We are not yet solving the problem! Hold them back from the solutions. If anyone offers a solution at any point you just ask them to hold that thought for a while. You will need the discipline of patience and politeness.

   3.1   How would we know we have succeeded in resolving this issue? Look at those impacts: financial, emotional, time and on the team.

   3.2   How would we measure that?

   3.3   How would we report that to ourselves?

4. **What's the Plan?**

   4.1   What are the choices of solutions we can develop? How do they each work against the success measures?

   - How achievable are they?
   - Does everyone agree on each solution?
   - Can they be done in time?
   - Does everyone understand the solutions?

   4.2   Is there a spectrum of choices across from one extreme to the other?

- Conservative to radical
- Cheap to expensive
- Difficult to simple
- Quick to slow.

4.3 Who wants to be accountable?
- Roles
- Responsibilities
- Milestones to consider along the way
- Resources.

5. **Let's check on the milestones and Accountabilities**

5.1 Measure, Monitor and Report

5.2 Challenge
- Go back to the beginning and think again
- Review it from another perspective
- Try and break it. Attack yourselves as if you are the enemy.

5.3 Design changes

5.4 Plan for the next review

5.5 Apply

Think about the decisions you need to make today and apply those questions. More often than not, they fit. Some decisions will have technical aspects, or people, markets, shareholders, and so on. You will learn to adapt this simple series of questions to those aspects.

Change your behaviour to change the behaviour of those around you:

Training your mind to do this, to apply the WISPA series of questions takes work. When you get it, it is the difference between 'good' and 'excellent'. What we are discussing here is changing your behaviour. We are talking about changing from being the manager who answers, to the leader who asks. This change is not something that will just happen. You will have to make a conscious decision to change the way you respond in each circumstance.

Like many things, changing your own behaviour requires that you apply a process:

1. What is the behaviour that you want to change from?
2. What is the behaviour that you want to change to?
3. How will you teach yourself to recognise the old behaviour?
4. How will you stop yourself?
5. How will you make yourself apply the preferred behaviour?

Once you start behaving differently, the people around you will also behave differently.

Their behaviour of going to you and asking what to do is something you have taught them. Every time they have come and asked for an answer you have automatically supplied it.

From now on, they are going to come to you and ask for your answer and you are going to reply with questions. You are going to WISPA to yourself.

Soon enough, they will stop coming to you with questions for you to answer. They will start coming to you with solutions. The change in your behaviour will have created a change in their behaviour.

Try it, practice it and measure the results.

So, let's do that. Apply the rules to your circumstance and talk about it at www.askingleader.com.

Designing a Series of Questions

How do we design a process to Ask a Series of Questions using **WISPA?**

1. **W**hat/why?
2. **I**mpacts?
3. **S**uccess?
4. **P**lan?
5. **A**ccountabilities?

The Asking Leader just needs to WISPA quietly to themselves to address many business decisions (and every impassioned argument with their daughters).

1. **What** is the background to an ASQ process?
    1.1 Where did this idea come from?
    1.2 How did it become an idea?
    1.3 What are we assuming here?
    1.4 What happens if we just ask a question and get an answer?
    1.5 Is there any advantage in developing a process, just to have a process?

1.6 Have you seen CEOs who haven't had a process? How did that work?

1.7 Are there any examples of a process we could look at? What was their success?

2. If we did design a process to ASQ, then what would be the **Impacts**?

2.1 Would it be a good use of time?

2.2 Will it develop better ideas?

2.3 Would we understand each other better?

2.4 How would it make us all feel?

2.5 Would it make us more money?

- Bring in more customers?
- Keep my good clients?
- Bring better shareholder relations?
- Get my business through the growth ceiling?

2.6 Will it help me develop better relations with people I am reluctant to deal with?

2.7 Can it help me identify better strategies for my business?

2.8 Do I need to think through decisions better?

2.9 Can I use it to keep my people accountable?

2.10 How can I introduce new ideas and practices to my business without getting too much resistance?

3. If we did design a process to ASQ, how would we know it was **Successful**? What would be the measures of:

3.1 Communication

3.2 Engagement

3.3 Good ideas and strategy

3.4 Customer satisfaction

3.5 Shareholder relations

3.6 Profit.

4. What will the process be? Will there be a **Plan** to implement?

   4.1 It will be a learning cycle

   - Each time we apply the process, we learn some more.

   4.2 It will have rules

   - That we can continually adapt.

   4.3 It will be guided by

   - Curiosity
   - Discipline.

5. We will all be **Accountable:**

   5.1 We will continually check-in with performance milestones.

   5.2 We will measure our performance and learn from each iteration of the learning cycle.

   5.3 We will use the process to create quality decisions from excellent content.

   5.4 We will celebrate successes.

   5.5 We will learn from objectives not yet met.

   5.6 If all fails, we will performance manage.

Later in the book I will show you Asking Leader questions for a variety of business aspects.

Developing the discussion

Oh, the decisions. The place where most CEOs want to start is at the end. The Asking Leader has the self-discipline to get to the end of the series to create great decisions with enormous engagement. The outcome of the process is the team must own the plan.

The **discussion** is the subset of the decision. It is divided by the steps of the WISPA process. Each step can be separately respected and thoroughly explored. The end game is the decision.

What are your suggestions to develop the discussion? Here are some of mine:

1. Manage the WISPA process to get the right content.

Rule No. 1: Only ever ask a question.

The challenge for the CEO is to not contribute to the discussion. Sure, you can manage the series and that may make some contribution to the discussion. However, (a big 'however') as the Asking Leader, you must put your contribution as a question.

For example, you will recognise that there is an important aspect of the issue that is not being discussed. Often, it is about the expense of the idea. Your challenge is to say,

'Are there other aspects of this issue that we should consider?'

Then, if you still don't get the answer you think the conversation needs – say, they haven't thought about the cost:

'What would be the financial implications of the idea?'

Make sure the content is only of the subsection of the process that you are in.

Rule: Fully complete each step before allowing the group to take the next step.

If you are asking about a deeper understanding of the issue, ensure that the discussion does not rush off to solutions. Slow them down. Keep the discussion about the subject of the moment.

2. Be a little bit bossy.

    Set your rules at the beginning and make them the rules for all your meetings. You are the CEO and that means you're the boss. We can be the boss with good humour. Your rules could be things like:

> Phones off – the first phone to ring buys the drinks
> Respect each view as though it were your own
> Don't repeat it – we heard you already
> Limit the discussion to the subject at hand
> Trust the process – we will get there
> Restate the values of your organisation
> Be honest and true to what you say
> Maintain the integrity of your words.

What are the rules of your meetings? What would you add or subtract from that list? Make your suggestions at www.Asking Leader.com.

3. Gather the **discussion** to create the **decisions:**

    3.1 End each step of the series with a summary of what you have heard.

    3.2 Conclude with a summary statement.

Make sure you **wrap up** the session with conclusions. This is where the Asking Leader becomes the CEO again. Your job is to conclude and make people accountable. Use WISPA.

What: 'From the discussion, the main points you have made are these ...'; 'We have decided the real issue is actually...'

Impacts: 'The issue is important because it ...'

Success: 'To resolve the issue we need to create success that looks like this ...'

Plan: 'The steps in the plan we have developed are these...'; 'We have set these milestones ...'

Accountabilities: 'X, Y and Z will deliver and report back by ...'

What is the issue?

The background to why we have suggested having some Asking Leader rules around the idea of Asking a Series of Questions is to learn. The ASQ rules are not hard and fast rules; they are meant to be broken. If we have some rules, we can try them, test them, stretch them, break them, and then rewrite them.

The rules are the process of learning.

It is often said that people learn by doing. The way to learn the ASQ is to get up on your feet and give it a go.

Rule No. 2: Plan the conversation.

The most important step is always the first. That step is to actually know what the issue is. Do you have the self-discipline to prepare for your conversations?

- What do I want to achieve from the conversation I am about to have?
- Why do I want to achieve that?

- Dig deeper and ask yourself that question again, why do I want to achieve that?
- Then go back to the beginning, what do I **really** want to achieve from this conversation?

Though a deeper understanding of the issue may seem like a waste of time, it is incredible how much time it saves to solve the correct problem.

If you don't take any other steps, if you just take this step, then you are getting past 'good'.

```
Rule No. 3: Get agreement on the issue.
```

If we have the discipline to apply ASQ rules, then we can actually test them in real time, think about how it worked and what we can do next.

What are the Impacts of having rules?

The impact of the idea of having rules is that ASQ becomes a learning method. The rules themselves are actually designed to be broken so that we continue to improve the process of ASQ.

Identifying and analysing the impacts of the issue takes true curiosity. You will have to inquire with your two ears and your one mouth – and in that proportion! You will have to listen hard. Not assume anything, make them say it out loud.

You will always need self-discipline to remain truly curious.

> Rule No. 4: Don't assume anything:
> make them say it out loud.

If we are going to have the discipline to be curious and inquisitive, then we have to apply the same discipline to the overarching idea.

It's a bit circular. Let's have some rules that we can apply, test, bust, rewrite and reapply. It is like we are back where we started, but we have lifted the bar on each revolution of the circle.

The learning cycle is something that usually makes CEOs feel good. CEOs love to learn and great CEOs love to see their people learn. The team, too, likes to learn. Learning in a group is a motivating and uniting practice that builds a positive company culture.

What indicates Success of the ASQ rules?

The goal of having rules is to be able to use them as a guide for further development. We should measure each revolution of the circle to determine our success. Success can be assessed by:

- the impact of the rules on your decisions and actions
- the number of times the rules are applied
- the number of people who are applying them
- further refinement of the ASQ rules.

> Rule No. 5: Clearly define success with numbers.

The success of the solution needs to be in as many numbers as possible. It can be in percentages or absolute numbers.

Go to www.askingleader.com for your contribution to the discussion.

 Try to avoid successes that are measured by how everyone feels. If everyone feels good, then develop a survey to assess that. Turn the 'feelings' into numbers.

How would we Plan to implement ASQ rules?

One way to do that would be to have a blog site where Asking Leaders could write in and tell of their experiences. They could offer their view on the application of the ASQ circle.

Rule No. 6: The plan is only as important as the agreement.

 A plan with no pre-existing agreement lacks ownership. The modern people will call it 'disempowerment'. I prefer to say that it is annoying and doesn't make people want to come to work and contribute.

If they agree on the plan and helped develop it, stand aside. They own it and they will do their best to make it happen.

Who is going to be Accountable for the delivery of the rules of ASQ?

Let's all be accountable. Let's all give it a go and report back in.

> Rule No. 7: They expect you to hold them to account.

You said you would do this. How are you going with it? Are we on track? Are we on time? Which steps of the plan are to be done by today? What support do you need to get to this step? What roadblocks have developed since the plan was devised?

The real issue here is what happens if you don't make them accountable.

 If you don't have the discipline to hold them to account because you are too busy, distracted or don't think it is worth following up, then your stocks are lowered. The staff will think less of you as a CEO.

There is a second way to think about accountability. That comes from Greg Bustin[4], a fellow Vistage Chair from the USA and the author of several books on the subject. In fact, he is a hero of mine.

Greg approaches the idea of accountability from the perspective that it is a **support system for winners**. He says that:

"Accountability is a choice. For everyone involved. That means when someone you've asked to do something makes a commitment and then fails to live up to that commitment, they are rewarded by their choice. Similarly, CEOs, owners, supervisors who tolerate behaviour by people who do not live up to their commitments are similarly rewarded by having chosen to tolerate this behaviour."

Throughout this book, we are going to discuss how to apply these rules of the Asking Leader to a range of normal business circumstances. However, if you only read this chapter, you will get the drift. If you want to learn more, you will read on.

---

4   Greg Bustin, *How Leaders Decide: A Timeless Guide to Making Tough Choices,* Sourcebooks, 2019

Listening

Asking questions is only one side of the equation. The other side is listening. Once we have asked the questions, we need to listen to the answers. I like to adapt Hugh Mackay's[5] statement that, "People are more likely to listen to us if we also listen to them". We should change the 'also' to 'first'. Then it becomes:

People are more likely to listen to us if we **first** listen to them.

The act of listening is both generous and patient. When you listen, you are generously giving the space and you are patiently giving the time to the other person. Imagine the self-discipline required to remain generous and patient. Often, listening is harder than asking.

One of the great leaders of all time, Sir Winston Churchill[6] was a great orator. He said:

---

5 Hugh Mackay, *Why don't people listen?* Macmillan Australia, 2013
6 Richard Langworth, *Churchill by Himself,* Elbury Press, UK, 2008

"Courage is what it takes to stand up and speak; courage is also what it takes to sit down and listen."

We could change Sir Winston's quote from 'courage' to 'self-discipline'.

'Courage is what it takes to stand up and speak; **Self-discipline** is what it takes to sit down and listen.'

All of us will be aware of the skill of listening. Do we have the discipline to practice that skill?

To have discipline, the Asking Leader needs to be a good listener. How do we discipline ourselves to listen well?

Personally, I am a butchers paper listener. I try to write down on the paper a quick and dirty summary of what each participant has said. Often, I will ask, 'I think you said this … Is that right?' That way:

1. the participants see that you have validated their thoughts
2. the ideas are there to refer to when you summarise.

Active Listening

For a CEO, the best guidance for listening is the concept of 'active listening'. We must develop the discipline to fully concentrate on what is being said – we have to listen with all of our senses.

Following are the component parts of active listening:

1. Presence

When in listening mode, the Asking Leader will have to be there. Fully. You need to lock out all your other thoughts and senses and intently focus on the discussion. You will need to be mindful of when your mind is wandering, your thoughts are elsewhere and you are distracted.

It is well-known that we can hear far more words per minute than we can speak. As a rough rule of thumb, we hear about three times more words than we can speak. This idle capacity in your brain is the trap that will allow you to lose focus.

Being present at the discussion gives the meeting the idea that you are intentionally listening without judgement.

2. Hearing

For me, listening is a challenge. I wear two rather heavy-duty hearing aids. My hearing is probably a result of my youth on bulldozers in the dust and heat of the outback. The constant squealing and squeaking of the tracks were probably the culprit. The tracks of a bulldozer are connected in a big heavy circle with steel pins that go through steel bushes. The pins were about 50 mm in diameter and about 300 mm long. That is a lot of steel rubbing on a lot more steel and it is loud.

This was in the 1970s when ear protection was either inadequate, unavailable or only for wimps.

Like many people who are hard of hearing, we learn to interpret both the voice and physical signals. Some deaf people can 'hear' very well. Deaf people are usually good at listening for what is unsaid. We can read the body and the intention and match it to the words that are coming out.

To make up for the lack of sound, we watch intently. If there is a disconnect, a person who struggles to hear well will see it quickly. We deaf people give the impression we are listening intently, but we are really watching intently.

We use our eyes with extra intensity to absorb as many of the signals as possible. Because I am so focussed, people often say that I clearly show that I am listening to them.

Sometimes we can see more than others will hear.

3. Physical listening

What you do with your body can affect how people answer your questions. If your body is saying that you are in an active position, then you can be perceived as interested and prepared to absorb their message. However, if you are passively sitting at the desk with your hands behind your head and your feet up on the table, the person answering your question will be turned off. They may even be offended. You have lost them.

Buy the dog.

If you are listening with a critical mindset it will show in your body. People can see when you are already preparing your response to their answer. If, on the other hand, you can show empathy they will see it and be far more honest in their answers.

Stephen Covey[7] said:

"Most people do not listen with the intent to understand; they listen with the intent to reply."

Have you ever caught yourself doing that? Waiting for that person to shut up so you can reply? Or worse, interrupting so you can reply.

---

7 Stephen R Covey, *7 Habits of Highly Effective People*, Simon & Schuster, New York, 2004

As Allan Pease[8] says, how you hold your hands is critical. Allan says that talking with the palms of your hands facing upwards shows that you are open. When your palms are facing down it is the opposite – it is an order or a power signal. Point your finger at them and then buy the dog.

Pease says, "your body language is an outward expression of your emotions". People can unconsciously read you and make instinctive decisions.

Do a little exercise with yourself. Stand in a conversation and observe the behaviours. Who is intent on replying and who is intent on understanding? What behaviours do those actions elicit from the speaker?

Then take it a step further. Watch yourself. Make a mental note of your normal behaviours. Are your behaviours adding value or taking value away from the conversations?

Again, it is difficult to teach yourself the physical listening skills. You may want to video yourself to try to see what other people see in you. Or have trusted colleagues give you a report on how they think you were perceived.

4. Listening filters

The real challenge is to correctly hear the messages you are receiving without using your own in-built filters. You will not hear properly if your filters shut down the receptors in your brain.

The filters are often about what you expect to hear. Or what you want to hear. You are anticipating the message and listening for the aspects that align with your own preconceived expectations.

---

8 Allan Pease, *Body language, the power is in the palm of your hands*, TEDx Macquarie University, 2013

More filters in your brain are hardwired from your culture. You will have certain beliefs and values that have been taught to you from your earliest days that will limit and alter the message that makes it to your brain. As people say things, your brain will be adjusting the message to meet the values and beliefs you have developed since birth. The little voice in your mind will be chatting away to make the adjustment for you.

Language can often be a filter. Even within your own language one single word can mean many things. When listening to an accent that you aren't familiar with, you may misinterpret the message again.

How you feel today will affect what you hear. Your current state of mind may be happy, sad, angry, anxious, or fearful. These feelings of today will change how you absorb the message. Imagine how you perform when you have not slept well. Imagine that grumpy feeling and how it will affect your capacity to absorb a message.

Each of these filters will echo in your head and reconstruct the messages that are being said. To manage these filters, the Asking Leader needs to 'be present'. The Asking Leader needs to really be there and concentrating on being fully receptive.

The skill of presence takes practice. Try it in your workplace. Try to listen with your filters turned off. Try to develop a level of curiosity that turns off the filters.

5. Managing what you hear

Once we understand and adopt the traits of active listening, the next step is to manage what comes next. I am continually confounded by the responses I get to questions. Sometimes they thrill me with insight, empathy and perspective. Other times they don't. How the Asking Leader responds determines the success of the discussion.

When we receive the thrilling responses, we should recognise them. There is not much more a CEO can do to motivate a team than to recognise them. We will talk more about recognition in Part 2.

How do you handle the discussion when it is not going forward? These are a few of the statements we have all heard:

1. 'Oh yeah but ...' or 'I really respect what you have just said, but ...'
2. 'I've been around a lot longer than everyone else and I can tell you from experience ...'
3. 'I suggested that last year and it was smashed down by the board!'

In the words of the great John Snow, King of the North, Master of Winterfell, Bastard son of Ned Stark,

"... everything that came before the word 'but' is bullshit."

6. Managing what you see

Then there is the body language of the participants. Some of your team are going to be extroverts who respond quickly. Some will be introverts who just want everyone to shut the heck up, so they can think. Others, the most difficult, are the passive-aggressive types who sit at the back with their arms folded and scowling smiles on their faces.

Asking Leaders will let the natural order take place. You will let the extroverts speak but limit how much and for how long. You will wait to ask the introverts. You will notify the introverts, 'I am going to ask your thoughts in a moment ...' I love the introverts because they have been thinking with their mouths shut. When they finally open them, the insights can be gold.

The passive-aggressive types are the most challenging. Often, they want to follow the wind and if they see that the room is absorbing the flow, they will soften. However, some dig in. If everyone is being positive and considering the day's challenge, their pre-existing view that they are right and everyone else is wrong may be confirmed.

My view is don't give them the oxygen. Don't ask them a question. Let them sit and stew. Confronting them will give them the air they yearn for – it will allow them to spill their aggression. Often it will be irrational. They will say things that conflate a range of issues into another and you will be unable to provide a rational response.

I learnt long ago that I cannot have a rational conversation with an irrational person. I learnt to take the long route around the objections that were boiling within.

7. Control yourself

You will find yourself closing in on solutions too quickly. You will need to learn to manage that instinct. Your brain is hardwired with a neural pathway that will close the questions down and jump to the solution or the agreement. Training your brain not to do that is to break a neural pathway. That break is not easy because your behaviour has become automatic.

I often ask CEOs to have a physical change. When they recognise they are exhibiting the wrong behaviour it is useful to have a physical change. To remind myself that I need to go back to WISPA, I often touch my lips with my index finger in the 'shhh' gesture. I am actually telling myself to shut the heck up and design the next question in the series. I have been learning a new neural pathway that is creating a learned leadership behaviour.

Rating – How good are you?

- If you had to give yourself a rating out of 10 for listening, where would you rate yourself?
- How do you rate yourself at asking open questions?
- How do you rate your presence, body language?
- How well can you turn off your listening filters?
- How well can you manage what you hear?
- If you got someone else to ask your Senior Leadership Team, Board, shareholders, key clients the same question, how would they rate you out of 10?
- Where would you like to be rated out of 10?
- What are you going to do about achieving that desired rating?
- How will we know that you have changed your behaviour?

Go to www.askingleader.com for your contribution to the discussion.

What comes next?

The next part of this book is about making the Learning Leader a real pathway for business leaders to follow. I have picked out only a few, but I think these are key aspects of business that apply in most places.

Part 2:

The Asking Leader Inside your Business

Company Culture

We can apply WISPA to understanding organisational culture.

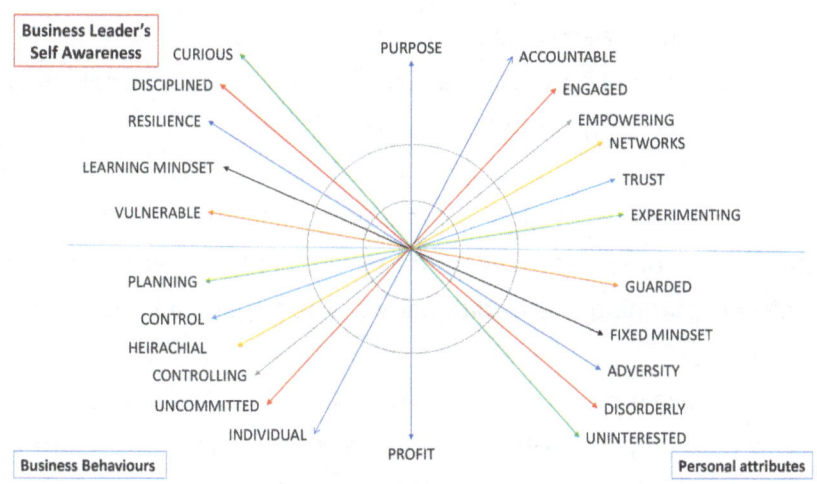

Figure 1 Asking Leader Mindset Shifts

Change your behaviour to change the behaviour of those around you

Company culture is how the company behaves. If you want to change the behaviours, you will need to start at the top. Simply, that is you.

If we go back to the earlier statement that if you first can change your own behaviour, then the behaviour of your team too will change.

Whatever behaviours you are exhibiting will be reflected in your company's culture.

I often challenge business leaders with the diagram above. I ask them to describe the personal attribute words. For example:

- What do those personal attributes mean to you?
- What are the impacts of you presenting as uninterested/guarded/etc?
- What are the impacts of you presenting as curious/vulnerable/etc?
- If you had to rate yourself out of 10, where would you put yourself on each of these lines?
- For you to change the culture in your company, what do you have to change about yourself?

Similarly, the structural organisation of the business has cultural impacts. The business behaviours of controlling, hierarchical and structured planning are traditional ways to organise your business structure.

These days those structures are seen as disempowering.

The new ways of networks, trust and experimentation are the current style of business organisation. In the same way, I ask the same style of questions:

- What do those business behaviours mean to you?
- What are the impacts of each?
- If you had to rate yourself out of 10, where would you put your business on each of those lines?

Now that you are an Asking Leader, what are the next questions that you would ask? I usually ask questions like:

- If you are there on those lines, where do you think you would like to be?
- If you moved along each of those lines, what would be the impacts of that change?
- What do you need to do to make those moves?
- How would we know you have made those changes in your own behaviours?
- If we monitor those changes, how would you like me to hold you accountable?

If we can get to this point, if we can get you, the CEO to change, then your company's culture too will change.

The next step is to engage your team.

What is the issue with company culture?

A company's culture, or how your company behaves, is the addition of its values and its purpose.

Culture = Values + Purpose

A lot of CEOs think that their company culture reflects their personal purpose and values. Often it is. But culture can be even bigger than that:

- Values are the beliefs that set the behaviours within the organisation.

- Purpose is a result of a group of people agreeing on some bigger ideas that drive them.

Culture is the addition of the values and the purpose. Culture is an amorphous aspect of any company that cannot be measured in absolute terms – but it can be measured.

When that works for you, it is gold. When it works against you, it can be a slow death. Culture is an intangible asset that has real value.

Culture affects the bottom line.

1. Values

Go on. Tell me. You have one of those company statements that declare your values. I'll bet it includes:

- honesty
- fairness
- ethical
- integrity
- sustainable
- excellence
- collaborative
- team
- community

and way more motherhood statements. What are yours?

Tell me, what does it mean? Did the company values change behaviours? Does it motivate staff to participate, contribute and engage? Does anyone in the company actually own this rubbish? Have we all seen these statements on the wall of companies which have a culture that can be best described as 'toxic'?

Is that the company that is full of Donna Do-Little and Darren Do-Nothing who blame management and the economy for every problem?

It would be an interesting statistic to find out if having company values has actually made any difference. Perhaps one of you can point us to a reputable study of that question.

If you get your company's values to align with the group behaviours that you call your employees, then there is real potential for a difference. You need to find their language from their lexicon and avoid the language of 'motherhood'.

2. Purpose

Are company values derived from the purpose of the organisation? Is the really big 'why' of why we are here in business, to do what it is that we do, the main source of company culture?

Refer again to Figure 1. The central line on the table is the line between profit and purpose. This line is the central theme of company culture.

The really successful companies that everyone quotes – such as Apple and Google – have clear statements of their purpose.

Back in the 1970s, Steve Jobs was inspirational. He said the purpose of Apple was:

"To make a contribution to the world by making tools for the mind that advance humankind."

Wow!

That is simple and inspirational! Who the heck has the gonads to say that they are going to advance humankind and actually sound credible? That statement inspired a whole generation of geeks to contribute to the advancement of humankind.

I have always been attracted to the old statement from Komatsu. In the days coming out of the Second World War, the Japanese approached business with a focus that was hell-bent on copying. They saw the big companies around the world and wanted to be them. Komatsu was (and is) the Japanese company that makes heavy construction equipment. Their target competition was the biggest and the best. Caterpillar. Their simple statement was:

"Encircle Caterpillar."

Imagine being the employee at Apple where you are going to advance humankind, or the employee at Komatsu where you are going to take on the world's biggest and best and beat them.

That is motivating!

Move forward thirty odd years and the statements are so bland that my eyes hurt, my body aches and I fall asleep.

Apple designs Macs, the best personal computers in the world, along with OS X, iLife, iWork and professional software. **Apple** leads the digital music revolution with its iPods and iTunes online store.

Komatsu says:

"Our vision is to become indispensable to our customers. We can achieve this by always being driven by our customer's success where every customer contact is an opportunity to enhance our brand value.

We will engage our employees to innovate and progressively earn the trust of our customers and sustainably grow the business for our shareholders."

When you are presented with these motherhood statements the energy is sucked from your day at work.

Or, you can encircle the 'Cat'. You can surround Caterpillar with products that are better, more powerful, reliable, cheaper, and win.

An excellent purpose statement is the old faithful from Woolworths:

Fresh Food People

A wonderful blend of marketing and motivation. In just three words!

The slogan says to the market that we are the people who supply you with fresh food. We are not a machine, we are people. We are a big company, but we are full of people who care about fresh food.

The statement is also a motivator for the people of the organisation. They like being part of the fresh food strategy. They like to present the food to show they care. It is a uniting concept that brings them together and sets a standard. This is then confirmed in their advertising. The ads show the people caring, smiling, fussing, presenting.

The statement is now thirty years old and still works with the market and with their people.

One of my clients who runs a pet store came up with: 'We love people who love their pets'. It says so much with so few words. We love pets, our people love pets, we love people who are pet people, if you love your pets, you will come to us.

And they do.

Why do we need a strong culture in our organisations? What's your experience? What are your needs?

What's your answer? Go to www.askingleader.com.

What are its Impacts?

If these companies can create a positive culture by developing shared values and purpose, then success is around the corner. It is funny how purpose creates profit – without focussing on profit, it comes. Deloitte wrote a paper on this in 2014[9]. They said:

- Organizations that focus beyond profits and instil a culture of purpose are more likely to find long-term success.
- Ninety-one per cent of respondents (executives and employees) who said their company had a strong sense of purpose also said their company had a history of strong financial performance.
- Yet employees (68 per cent) and executives (66 per cent) believed that businesses were not doing enough to instil in

---

9 Deloitte, *Culture of Purpose*, 2014

their culture a sense of purpose aimed at making a positive impact on all stakeholders.

Lisa McLeod[10] says that 51 per cent of your workforce is not engaged. Half of them are just going through the motions, and the other half have signed on and are committed to your needs.

Often these places are either government departments or high-pressure organisations, which are entirely profit-driven. Lisa McLeod says it clearly when she says:

"Profit doesn't drive purpose. Purpose drives profit."

Doubtless, these engagement levels are affecting productivity. Productivity creates profit.

We have all been in workplaces where the lack of commitment from some people just drains the energy from the place. Those workplaces that feel flat and lifeless are usually a result of poor culture. They have no purpose and they own no values. The poor culture that is derived from the lack of energy makes for an unhappy day at work. No one cares, no one gives a shit.

'Is it 5 o'clock yet?'

'Let someone else answer the phone. It isn't my job.'

'It's all her/his fault'.

'I blame management.'

'I did a great report and they complained about the font.'

---

10 Lisa Earle McLeod, *Leading with Noble Purpose: How to Create a Tribe of True Believers*, Wiley, USA, 2016

Would you want to stay working in that place? If another job comes up, you are going to take it. Employee retention rates are going to be lower than your industry's standard and those who leave are going to tell all of their colleagues.

When you walk around your office and find that half your employees are looking at LinkedIn, you know you have a problem.

The importance of coffee ...

I once was a Director of an organisation where Workplace Health and Safety (WHS) was taken very seriously. The next most important thing was coffee.

I was Chair of the Audit and Finance Committee (A&F) and we had just completed the transfer to new offices. Of course, the office needed a fit-out and the capital expenditure required the oversight of the A&F Committee. We were consulted on every detail of office chairs, wireless communication devices, filing systems, departmental layouts. There was much gnashing of teeth over the most minor details.

The most amusing was the blatant use of the WHS process to get whatever it was that they wanted. They wanted coffee. And WHS was very important!

They wanted two very expensive all singing, all dancing, Italian coffee machines that made coffee that would normally be only available from the trendy neighbourhood café made by a heavily-tattooed, bearded, Italian hipster barista. As Chair of the A&F, my duty was to point out that these machines were extraordinarily expensive. "Perhaps," I asked of the three senior executives who were tasked to get this expenditure through the A&F, "we only need one of these machines?"

They looked at me with straight faces. Prepared as they were for this question. With much consternation they advised me that the WHS audit had advised that it was unsafe to walk down the internal stairs with a cup of scalding hot coffee. It was therefore safest to have two expensive Italian coffee machines. In unison they nodded with a look of scholarly agreement. Not a glimmer of humour as they rubbed their chins and agreed on the importance of this critical safety measure. They advised me that the safety auditor had been quite firm on this point.

I looked outside the meeting room to the smart staircase that was of such concern. It went down only one level. Immediately beside the staircase was the lift.

"That's no worries," I said suppressing my smug smile. They looked momentarily relieved. "We will just have to mandate that everyone who makes a coffee has to use the lift on the way back down."

You know what happened. You have seen this before.

I had to back down. They got their bloody coffee machines. In the interests of avoiding a revolt, I had to acquiesce. (But you all know the first rule of negotiations. Never make a concession without asking for a matching concession. They didn't get the fancy new computers they wanted … Well, not immediately anyhow.)

The impacts of a poor culture are:

- profit
- productivity
- employee retention.

What else do you think are the impacts of poor organisational culture?

65

Measuring Success

If we can improve our organisation's culture, how would we know we have succeeded?

Success can be measured by:

1. Job satisfaction
2. Employee retention Productivity
3. Profit
4. Behaviours.

Probably one of the first things that your people will start doing is talking up their role in the organisation and the organisation itself. Perhaps there is a way to measure that. A survey of job satisfaction could do it. Or perhaps you will just feel it in the workplace.

Your monthly one-on-one conversations may be different. You may be able to judge the feel of the workplace there. You may be able to design questions in that conversation to get a feel for how it is going. It could be as simple as: 'How does the workplace feel lately?'

The next level will be employee retention. You will start to see employees wanting to stay. This is a longer-term measure, but it may be noticeable in twelve months. You will need a benchmark figure to compare it to. What is your employee retention now? How long have they been there and what percentage of turnover do you have? With the right culture, you will move those numbers up so far that you can measure them.

The third level of success for a positive workplace culture will be in productivity. It will start with ideas from the floor. You will hear: 'I think we could make this activity efficient/easier/cheaper/quicker if we did this ...' You will also hear: 'If I helped you with that, then we could make both our jobs more efficient/easier/cheaper/quicker.'

That is what you will hear. But you need to measure the impact. That will be in productivity. Each company will have its own measure of tonnes/hour, widgets/day, contracts, sales, labour/unit and so on.

The important measure is profit. Good companies make profits. It is far easier to make profits in good places to work. Sales will be up, and costs will be down.

The final measure is behaviour. I like to think of behaviours in three categories. There are behaviours that are not acceptable in your organisation and they will be ruled as 'below the line.' Then there are behaviours that are acceptable. They can be ruled as 'above the line.' Really, what we are looking for are behaviours that your organisation, 'encourages or aspires to.'

How do you measure the success of your company's culture?

www.askingleader.com

Planning your series of questions to measure success

If the measures are employee satisfaction, productivity and profit, how do we get there? As always, it's ASQ. Ask a series of questions that will challenge our staff to build a better workplace.

What is the series of questions we should ask our staff?

The first ideas that come to the mind of many speakers and writers in this arena are the ones that employees want:

- to feel valued
- to make a difference
- to be part of something that is making change for good.

As Simon Sinek[11] says, people want to understand why the company is in business and why their role is part of that. He says:

"People don't buy what you do; they buy why you do it."

Sinek gives the example of the Wright Brothers and their first flight. Imagine working for no money, with no resources, in a paddock in front of no one to build the first flying machine. Those people were not there for the money; they were there because they understood the 'why'.

There is a strong argument about the much-maligned millennials. They change jobs more often than previous generations. They seem to have the loyalty of an alley cat. They want to start their role in your organisation in your seat. They no longer answer the question of 'What do you want to achieve in the organisation?' with 'I want to work my way up to sit in your seat.' They now say: 'Get out of the way, I will sit just there, right now thank you. OMG, as if I would start somewhere else. BTW, close the door on your way out. Milk, no sugar.'

This group of millennials are particularly motivated by the 'why'. They are deeply connected to any number of social movements based around their personal values. As Patrice Thompson[12] says in her eloquent TED talk, "the millennials are bold, opinionated and not afraid to speak up".

She also says that the keys to engaging millennial staff are:

---

11 Simon Sinek, *Start with Why*, Portfolio, New York, 2009

12 Patrice Thompson, *A millennial's proposal for a happy multigenerational workplace*, TED Institute, 2014

- collaborative projects
- cross-training so that people learn from each other
- rewarding and recognising valuable ideas.

I am a grumpy old Baby Boomer who was brought up on loyalty, duty and selflessness. I struggle to understand these different perspectives. I know I have to.

For people in your organisation to feel valued, that they are making a difference and are part of something, you need to ask them …

1. 'Why' questions (not what we do, or how we do it, but why)
    1.1 What do we do that is important in society?
        - How do we make a difference?
        - Why is that difference important to society?
        - Why are we here doing this?
    1.2 What do you do in your role that makes a difference?
        - What aspect of your role is important?
        - Where does your role have an impact?
    1.3 How do you make a difference?
        - How do you contribute to making a difference?
    1.4 When everything is going well, what do you love most about your job?
        - Is there something that motivates you to contribute?
2. Collate a list of the statements that you think resonate with them:
    2.1 It could be a snowboard of sticky notes that you then group
    2.2 A survey
    2.3 Group reporting.
3. Distil the lists into statements of:
    3.1 Purpose
        - We are here because …

3.2 Values
- We believe in …

4. Set goals around the statements:

4.1 Brief – not more than ten words

4.2 Brave – not motherhood.

5. Distribute again for feedback:

5.1 Ask how this will be adopted

5.2 Ask how we will know it is working

5.3 Ask what we need to do to support it

5.4 Ask when we should review it.

A great way to get a measure of your culture is to ask your people to fill out this form from Colin Chodos of Corporate Connection Strategies.

Colin Chodos

Culture Analysis.

How do you rate your company culture?	Your rating 1-10	Your desired rating 1-10	Actions to improve the culture and teamwork
Collaboration			
Openness			
Challenge openly			
Socialisation			
Vulnerability			

How do you rate your company culture?	Your rating 1-10	Your desired rating 1-10	Actions to improve the culture and teamwork
Sharing of information			
Laughter			
Critique			
True Support for each other			
Modelling of company values			
Is Leadership behaviour championed?			
Critical thinking – explore the options			
Trust			
Common goal – if you ask 20 people would they agree?			
Accountability			
Blame			

How do you rate your company culture?	Your rating 1-10	Your desired rating 1-10	Actions to improve the culture and teamwork
Inspiring others			
Culture of recognition			
Culture of a learning organisation			
Culture of coaching			
Strategic thinking			
Service ethic			
Commercial culture of profitability			

Ensuring Accountability

Review the statements.

1. Check on the measures
2. Discuss the implementation
3. Celebrate any successes.

Repeat.

The weakest link

I always wanted to have a good culture in my workplace. I had just assumed that my enthusiasm would affect the people around me. Being so young and energetic, there was no way that people wouldn't be motivated with me. I demonstrated my enthusiasm by hard work. We just got in and did it. Well into the nights and through the horrific heat of the northern NSW summer. We ate the dust of many harvests, covered in layers of grease from our machinery and our sweat. We battled horrific natural events of floods and fires and we endured droughts and low prices. We got kicked by rogue calves, thrown from tired horses, broke limbs and our hands bled from the wear. My hands today are a wonder of the repairing power of scar tissue.

Surely everyone would find that exciting and motivating? The wonderful opportunity to be hot, sweaty, dirty, and injured was all anyone could want. I was sure that we had a really strong company culture.

Feeling a bit sure of myself, I employed a HR consultant to come in and develop the capacity of my staff to lead their teams. I was in the fortunate position of not needing that help myself because I was already the leader.

You know where this is going.

It was me who was the weakest link in the chain.

I soon discovered that my teams often wanted me to bugger off out of their way and let them get it done without being distracted by my endless stream of ideas, objectives, tasks, and challenges. They said that I would often fly in, get a job half-done and then leave the rest to them. They said I had good ideas, but so did they – and I hadn't taken the time to listen to them.

I took their feedback with dignity, admitted my errors and declared a new way. Later, in a private moment, I was very hurt.

I had learnt that we didn't have a good culture, and it was my fault. I had to learn another way. I had to have the discipline to learn that new way. I had to learn to be more inclusive in developing the ideas and solutions and less intrusive in the day-to-day roles. I used that as a little personal mantra for a while – more inclusive and less intrusive.

First, I had to change, so the people around me could change.

It is lessons like these that make us – as CEOs – conscious of the loneliness of our role.

What has been your experience in developing a company culture? www.askingleader.com

Human Relations—
The biggest problem
and the biggest
solution in business

Human relations have been an issue since the industrial revolution. In the cotton mills of Liverpool and Manchester, the workers were just cogs in a wheel. They were not required to think, just to do. They were expected to perform a menial and repetitive task in conditions of poor light, deficient ventilation and terrible safety.

You will have heard the term 'Luddite'. It refers to people who resist change and the introduction of new technology.

In 1812, some of a group of Luddites broke into a textile plant and smashed the new machinery. There was then a protest of some 2,000 workers. The factory managers responded with firearms and three of the protesters were killed and 18 wounded.

It was a salient lesson about the introduction and management of new technologies. The lesson is still useful today – except the shooting part!

How do we, as CEOs, introduce new ideas, methods and systems to make our business more sustainable and profitable? And then, how do we do that without disaffecting our employees?

Most of my CEO clients cite HR as their biggest challenge. We have all heard it – often from our own mouths:

- you can't get good people
- there's no loyalty anymore
- my staff want to go home more rested than when they came to work
- I feel like I am working for them – it is my house on the line to keep them in a job
- I did not get one suitable applicant for the role I advertised
- I've got one bad apple and he/she is poisoning the whole group
- I've spoken to that employee and he/she just doesn't get it
- we have job descriptions, but no one wants to be accountable for anything.

What have you heard? www.askingleader.com

Some theories around motivation

1. Transparency and self-directed teams

When I was doing my university degree, I studied Organisational Behaviour. This was the late 1970s and we thought it was pretty damned sophisticated. Later, it was Ricardo Semler in his book *Maverick* who got to me to think about HR. He changed his whole manufacturing and sales business to 'self-directed work teams'. He downgraded (or sacked) everyone with the title of 'manager' and said to each team, 'You work it out.'

Semler then let his HR team wither away and leave. Soon enough, he had no HR people on the team, and he had complete harmony and excellent productivity. This is a quick summary of his approach.

The business revolution

- Employees, acting as partners and associates, make all their own decisions.
- They evaluate their managers every six months.
- They're even encouraged to start their own companies.
- Potential managers are interviewed by the people who will be working for them.
- All have access to company books.
- No first-class and second-class citizens.
- Managers set their own salaries, bonuses.
- No formality: a minimum of meetings, approvals and memos.
- Shopfloor workers set their own productivity targets and schedules.
- Managers take turns to operate as chief executive.
- "The truly modern company avoids an obsession with technology and puts quality of life first."

If you read through that list about how it would apply in your workplace, what does it make you think?

Semler introduces a level of **transparency** that nearly all CEOs will find challenging. He would leave a couple of board seats open for anyone who wanted to come along and participate. Even the cleaner could come in.

He challenges the idea of **control**. The CEO doesn't make the decisions – you all do. You decide who your manager is. The managers decide what their pay is.

He challenges the idea that technology is more important than the **quality** of life.

By thinking differently about how we engage and manage our people, we can create harmony and productivity.

Many will find Semler too challenging. A bridge too far. What I want you to do is absorb the direction he is taking. His pathway to **engagement** is something we can challenge ourselves with. I think it is higher-order thinking; you may think he is nuts. We are probably both right.

2. Sources of satisfaction

Motivation became a focal point in the organisation behavioural thinking. A range of theories emerged in the 1950s and 1960s and include theories from notable researchers such as: Frederick Herzberg, Abraham Maslow, David McClelland, Victor Vroom, and Douglas McGregor. These theories underline employee motivation, work performance, and job satisfaction.

We studied Frederick Taylor. He was the bloke who worked out what was the correct-sized shovel to move coal. Then we went onto Elton Mayo who concluded that job performance was strongly correlated to social relationships and job content.

My favourite is Herzberg. He was an American psychologist who developed his idea of Motivator-Hygiene Theory. He was described as the 'Father of Job Enrichment'. His analysis is summarised for the most part in the chart below.

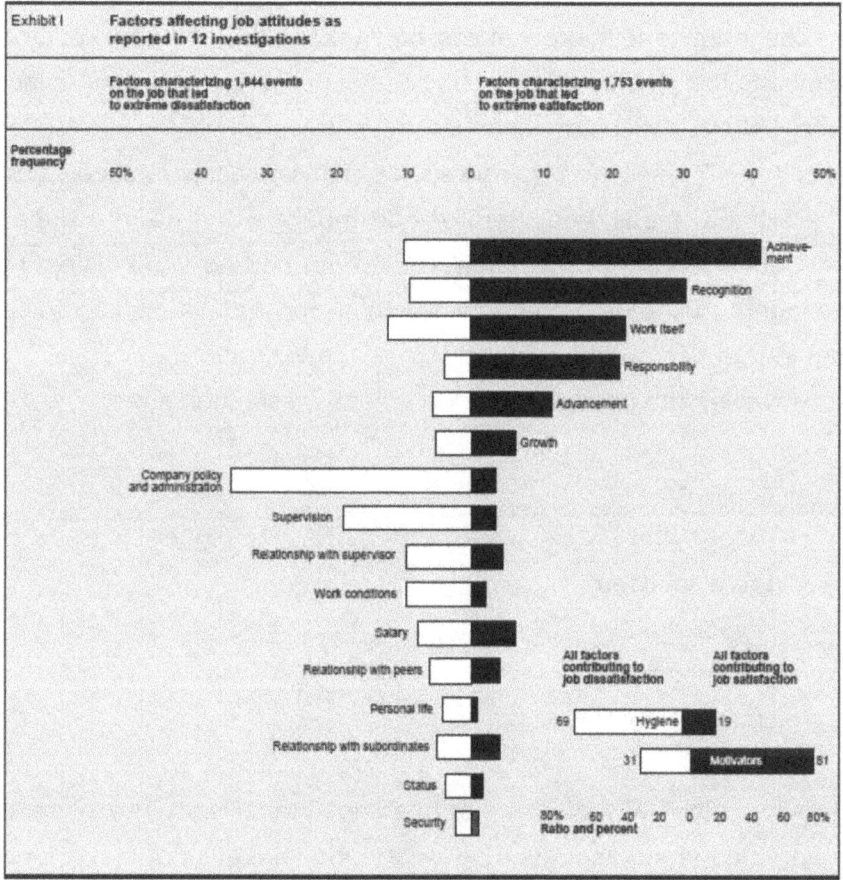

Figure 2 Herzberg's Motivator-Hygiene Theory

I carry this chart with me everywhere. I often show it to clients as a way to understand the decisions they are considering.

Herzberg describes the two paradigms of the chart as Hygiene and Motivators. Hygiene really only keeps you clean, and Motivators are what engage you in your role at work. The chart shows that 'salary' is not an outstanding motivator – and is actually the source of more dissatisfaction than satisfaction. Then why do we always defer to salary as the way to get our staff engaged?

79

The dominant source of dissatisfaction is 'Company Policy & Administration'. There is virtually no hope of policy as a motivator. In fact, every time management announces more rules, employee satisfaction goes down. The second dominant source of dissatisfaction is 'Supervision'.

Perhaps this is what Semler had meant when he introduced his 'Self-Directed Work Teams'. His model had no supervision, no managers and no HR professionals writing long and detailed contracts that introduced company policies and administration.

However, the headings that do create satisfaction are:

- achievement
- recognition
- the work itself
- responsibility
- advancement
- growth.

When I look at that group of headings I think 'soft'. These are all intangible human aspects that are emotional. Let's put statements to each of them:

- Achievement
  - 'I feel good when I achieve a goal that I have set for myself.'
- Recognition
  - 'If my workmates and supervisors see that I have done well, it makes me feel good that they say so.'
- The work itself
  - 'I like mastering my craft. I like being good at what I do.'
- Responsibility
  - 'I do care. I want to own my role and deliver to that.'

- Advancement
  - 'I am good at my job, and I want to continually get better at it. I want to go up to the next level.'
- Growth
  - 'I want to learn and grow in my role.'

Not one person is saying, 'I want to be paid a commission to make me work harder and better'. Or 'give me some very narrow boundaries within which I will work and I will perform well – I love rules'.

Thinking differently about the value-add of HR

CEOs are always mindful of the trade-off between efficiency and effectiveness. We have to run our businesses efficiently, but in the not-for-profit sector where you are reporting to stakeholders like government or members, then often the efficiency measures lower the effectiveness of the organisation.

Not unlike the success measures in the company culture, success in HR is around:

- employee retention
- job satisfaction
- productivity
- profit.

Employee retention is easy to measure. Another way to look at it is Staff Retention. Whatever you call it is right.

Job satisfaction is more subjective. However you measure job satisfaction, there is an element of 'feel'. Larger companies can do surveys and bring in consultants to give an objective measure of a subjective challenge. Does the workplace feel good? Are the staff engaged in their roles and in making a contribution to the company? These are often immeasurables.

Productivity as a measure is pretty easy but it is often not done well. In my experience it is often confusing for CEOs to find the exact measure that works best for their company and industry.

In farming, we used to talk about yield per hectare. However, our limiting factor was water. The productivity measure should have been yield per millimetre of available moisture. What is your limiting factor and how can you develop a productivity measure that shines a clear light on it? Is it tonnes per hour, or is it documents, or sales per person, and so on?

Profit is pretty easy. It is like anything else, if you implement a change you will always want to measure the impact of that change. The ultimate measure in our businesses is usually profit. However, in a not-for-profit entity, the measure may be more simply about effectiveness.

What is your HR team doing now?

1. Compliance

Are they:

- keeping you out of jail
- limiting the fines
- ensuring that if you are tested in court you will have a reasonable defence
- fattening the lawyers
- keeping a filing cabinet full of paper that protects the shareholders.

It is a pity that our (litigious) society has developed the need for such protection. Every board director worth their salt will focus on compliance as one of their four main roles (the others being strategy, monitoring performance and appointing you – the CEO.)

The HR team are mostly arse-covering when they could be adding value.

What are the Impacts?

Productivity. Management time. Jail. Cost. Replacement.

We are all aware of the **energy** a 'bad apple' can take. I have had many clients who have vacillated between 'sack the bastard' and 'let's just see what happens'. I have done it myself. I'll bet you have too. The amount of energy, time, angst, and thrashing around in bed at night over the 'bad apple' is not good. It is time and energy that would be better spent identifying opportunities, talking with key clients, scoping out prospects, attracting a new investor.

The secondary impact of HR is **productivity**. There is no doubt in the mind of every CEO that Human Relations is the difference between a productive and a not-so-productive workforce. The macro scale of human relations is the company culture. The micro scale is the individual relationship the company has with each employee. The intangible link between the two scales of human relations can make for a productive workforce.

Another impact of HR is **engagement**. When you ask for input, are they engaged? Do they want to contribute? Are they clock-watchers who want to get out the door on the stroke of 5 pm? Engagement is one of the key outcomes for the Asking Leader. When the Asking

Leader asks for involvement, do they spring to life and become motivated by the discussion?

Finally, there is the **cost**. I have often heard it said that replacing a staff member is very expensive. Some estimates are 40 per cent of the annual salary. Especially when you consider:

- the cost of delaying the decision to replace someone
- the cost of that person not performing well
- the cost of replacing them
- getting them onboard to perform in their role, then it may well be more than 40 per cent.

If you have ten staff who average $100,000 and you lose two each year, you just took $80,000 from your bottom line. I reckon it's more than that.

Plan

My clients have been developing the understanding that human relations is a big beast with several facets. We have found using the overarching ethic of the Asking Leader to engage and involve staff is easier. Then we break that down into the facets of HR. They are:

- job descriptions
- interviews
- on boarding/introduction/induction
- reviews/discussions
- performance management
- exit interviews.

1. Job Descriptions

These are the core of HR. If you get the job description right, then the rest of the task falls more easily into place. A job description that engages the candidate with the values and purpose (culture) of the company from the beginning usually attracts the right candidate. If the job description can explain why the company is here and why this role supports the purpose of the company, then the candidate can align their own values into that description. The 'buy-in' begins from the very first sentence of the job description.

The next step of the job description is to describe the objectives or goals of the role. The job description should have three to five objectives that have nice measurable numbers on them. You will increase sales by xx per cent, you will grow our market share by xx per cent, you will increase the efficiency of our plant by xx per cent, you will reposition our company at the top.

Right there you have the beginnings of the performance reviews that happen each month. You have set the standard. The difference in this approach is that you have not told them 'how' to do the job. You have told them what you want them to achieve in the role. This is very important when we talk about interviewing (next).

Lastly, the job description should describe the type of person you are looking for. You could think about it as, 'What are the personal attributes I would like to see in this role?' What are the personal skills they should bring to the table on interview day? Should they be prompt, efficient, attention to detail, big picture person, tough, communicator … and so on?'

Kim Seeling-Smith of Ignite Global describes this as the 'PGS' job description:

Purpose

Goals

Strengths.

What is not in that job description?

There is no 'how'. The job description is not a work plan of how you are to do your job, it is an objective plan of what the job is to achieve. It is an important difference that allows the Asking Leader to expand upon during the interview and afterwards in subsequent conversations. The Asking Leader will be able to ask a series of questions to empower and engage each employee based on their job descriptions.

Get the job description right, and you are nearly there.

2. Interviewing

The first stage of the interviewing process is to decide who to interview. It is damned easy to miss a good candidate if you are not sufficiently diligent in your screening process. It is very hard to see the strengths of passion, dedication and commitment in a written document. Some people are not good at writing that down – and others write it down and don't actually possess those strengths.

Interviews are the outcome of the job description. A good interview starts from a good job description.

A good interview is water off a duck's back for the Asking Leader. It is only about asking questions. The questions you ask are to elicit only one response.

Evidence

If you design your series of questions correctly you will be asking each candidate for evidence that they meet your criteria. You want evidence that you can check. You want evidence that your candidate is who they say they are:

You want to know that your purpose and their **purpose** aligns.

They have experience and demonstrated capacity to deliver against the **goals** of the role.

They have the **strengths** and attributes of the person you are looking for.

The way to get the evidence is to ask questions that are open: 'Tell me about your experience in improving sales.' 'How have you managed difficult employees in the past?' 'How have you interacted with a team in your previous roles?'

Don't ask closed questions that telegraph your preferred answer: 'We need to improve sales, are you able to do that?'

'Yes'

'Good, start Monday?'

Don't ask those smart-arsed questions that you can download on Pinterest: 'What are your greatest weaknesses?' 'Of all of our candidates—and we have 34—why should we hire you?' 'Where do you see yourself in five years?' These are not questions that are going to help you be sure you have the candidate you need to meet the objectives and fill the role you have designed.

They do make the candidate squirm – and that can be fun if you are that type of person.

You can ask general questions about their strengths and these can be a little hidden. For example, one of my favourites is, 'Tell me about someone whose career you have helped.'

A 'giver' will tell you about someone lower than them. 'I helped a young person who was new to our industry get over the first steps of their career. He/she went on to become a really important part of that business.'

A 'taker' will tell you about someone higher than them. 'I helped my sales manager become the new CEO. He/she wouldn't be there today without me.'

That question has the capacity to elicit an evidence-based response.

Design the interview to draw out the evidence that the candidate will:

1. Align with your purpose and be a good fit in your organisation
   - Understand their values and drivers
   - Find if they will be motivated by your values and drivers
   - Understand their organisational fit.
2. Test their experience and capacity to deliver the goals
   - Find any successes or learnings in their past experience
   - Understand their capacity to meet the goals
   - Do their skillsets match the need?
3. Find the type of person you are looking for
   - Aptitude
   - Attitude.

It's all about the attitude!

One of my crusty old farm managers used to proffer advice to all about him without too much encouragement. He was a wily old bugger who was an excellent judge of character. He was one of those blokes who created a nickname for everyone and had a good turn of phrase that could simply explain a situation.

My favourite nickname that he gave our grader driver was 'Lantern'. We would all ask why this poor old bastard was called the Lantern. He would reply: 'Well, he is quite dull. And you have to carry him.'

He was quite a tough farm manager who gave little room for error from his team. One mistake was not that good, but he could get through it. However, if they made the same mistake twice then they were slow learners and perhaps they should take the opportunity to work elsewhere.

He would say that, 'If they have the right attitude, I could teach them the skills. If they have the skills and the wrong attitude, I can't help them'.

It's a simple analogy, but it's accurate. In a job description and during an interview we often focus on the skillset. Skills are important. The deeper need for the Asking Leader is to find out whether the candidate can:

- learn
- grow
- adapt
- work in a team
- listen
- be curious
- have self-discipline
- work out solutions rather than focus on the problems
- be responsible for their work and own it
- believe in where your company is going is where they want to go.

These attitude issues are all part of the 'Strengths' portion of the job description. The Asking Leader will work out ways to ask questions that show evidence of the attributes that you have decided are critical to fill the role.

3. On Boarding – off to a good start

Everyone in the HR department thinks that the purpose of the on boarding period is to manage the risks. It is all the things on the left side of the Herzberg chart. It is to introduce:

- Workplace Health & Safety procedures
- company policies that cover sticky and difficult subjects such as harassment, presentation and behaviour.
- company policies on all things financial such as payment, personal expenses
- the rest of the team.

On the list goes.

The HR department is right. That is their job. Most of us crusty old bastards would think that they have just been employed to document what was once called 'common sense'.

That is not your job. You are the CEO. You do need to know the compliance side is done well. Your job is different. Your job is to get the best performance from your shiny new staff member.

Your new team member has a job description and now they need a work plan. The Asking Leader will ask the question:

'How are you going to achieve the work goals you have in the job description?'

The Asking Leader will then listen as their shiny new employee sets their own objectives and measurables for the foreseeable future. It will have tidy little timelines and metrics that we can all talk about later.

Many job descriptions include the work plan. This one doesn't. We are not going to tell you what to do; we are going to ask you what you will do to achieve the goals? It will be your plan and not mine. You will 'own' the plan and we will help you achieve it. This approach is a little bit of Ricardo Semler's approach.

The job description may say, 'Increase sales by twenty per cent and maintain our 15 per cent margin.' The Asking Leader will ask 'What is your plan to achieve that target?'

The response should be the work plan. 'I will need to increase our sales conversion rates by 15 per cent. We will need to improve our accuracy in our advertising and develop a more consistent message that aligns with customer needs. We will need to do some training and measure the changes.' And so on.

The shiny new employee probably just told you what you would have told them anyway. Or, they just told you some things you hadn't even considered. They will often give you some golden insights that come from their perspective and experience.

Take it. Write it down. Welcome them on board. 'Let's talk again in a month and we can see how you're going.'

Then we have the basis of performance monitoring.

4. Effective Performance Monitoring

This is not performance management. That is something else when things are not going well. Performance monitoring is getting it done before that happens. I call these meetings **1:2:1s**. They are the opportunity for the Asking Leader to sit on a one-to-one basis and ask questions.

The 1:2:1 is the chance for you to (as Kim Seeling-Smith says in her book *Mind Reading for Managers*):

1. Get feedback
2. Discuss the objectives of the role
3. Talk about their career

4. Develop their underlying motivators
5. Build their strengths.

The Asking Leader will have the discipline to keep to a calendar of these conversations. The Asking Leader will need the curiosity to continually dig deeper into the mind of the employee. That is why Kim Seeling-Smith calls it 'mind reading'.

The Asking Leader will regard these conversations as a constructive use of time. You will do this by framing the conversations around the notion that the purpose of these 1:2:1s is to help them achieve their objectives and to grow.

1. The **Feedback** conversation should be about asking really simple and open questions. How are you going? What are you seeing? How are you fitting in? What are you thinking about that you think I should know? What are you hearing in the marketplace?
   There is nothing measurable and uncomfortable about this conversation. It gets them in the frame of mind where their views are valued. You may also want to disseminate some company news. The board has decided that we are going to invest in a new plant. We have to cut back here.
   Again, nothing that they probably don't know already. Every piece of news that you give will be seen through their prism of 'How will that affect me?'
   This conversation should be had monthly at least – if not more often.
2. The **Objectives** conversation is more pointed. The Asking Leader will bring out the Job Description and discuss how we are going against the objectives. It is important that your role here is to help them achieve the objectives. You are in this together and your objectives are aligned with theirs.

The Asking Leader will ask, 'how are you going with your sales system? What have you put in place to improve the conversion ratio? What have you learnt from that? How do we need to adapt? What support do you need? Should we adjust the target (up or down)?'

The Objectives discussion can happen as often as you think is necessary. Some, particularly in sales, should happen weekly. Others with slow and longer time frames can happen every two months. I would think you would not want to go too far beyond quarterly.

I think the old idea of discussing this yearly is negligent. It is an important aspect. The Asking Leader will want to be closer to the issues and opportunities.

3. The **Career** discussion can happen less regularly. I encourage Asking Leaders to hold them every six months. Maybe yearly after they have been there a few years.

    The underlying subtext of the career discussion is: 'How can I build you up to take the next step in your career?' 'What are you seeing in your role that you want to know more about?' 'Is there training you have identified?' 'What connections do you want to make in our industry?'

    This idea is counterintuitive. You are building them up to leave you – and they may. If you are good, they will not leave you. If they are not good enough, they will leave you.

4. **Developing their underlying motivators** is really about their values. What gets them out of bed each morning? What is important to them and how does that align with their day-to-day role? What are they doing outside of work that really interests them? If you're running a coal mine and your shiny new employee has become an avid member of an anti-coalmining group, you may deduce that you have a problem. Conversely, they may have

become really interested in new technologies in how to reduce your coal mine's environmental impact.

This type of discussion may only need to happen every year. However, you may sometimes develop a sense that the motivation level is dropping, and it is time to discuss it.

5. The final conversation is about their **Strengths.** Again, these are listed in the original job description and may be worth reviewing. It may be that you have an employee who doesn't exactly fit the list and needs development in one or more areas. It may also be that your shiny new employee is over-achieving in one area and that will be worth recognising.

5. Performance Management

Performance management is when the wheels are coming off. All CEOs have done this. We have done it poorly – but every now and then we have got it right.

I've often tried the 'shit sandwich' approach – and it never worked. I would give some good news, then some bad news, then some good news. All I ever succeeded in doing was confusing them. They didn't know whether they were getting a pat on the back or a kick up the arse. The real purpose was to kick them up the arse! It is better to just do that.

I suggest that this not be a 1:2:1. You should bring a third (and independent) party to sit in on the meeting. By having a third person in the room it becomes more difficult for the employee to conflate extraneous issues that are not directly about their poor performance. The third person becomes a witness that the issues are properly addressed.

I have had many situations where the poor performing employee claimed: sexism, racism, 'that person has always been jealous of me', 'it's not my fault', and that 'you have never liked me anyway'.

When I was developing the name the 'Asking Leader' I put it to one of my clients for feedback. A quick-witted bloke with a wicked humour, he quickly replied 'Oh, the Arse King Leader'. It sounded very funny at the time, but we started to play with the joke a bit further.

I was then reminded how some of our group always respond to each problem with a solution. If an employee comes through the door with a problem, then my client would solve it (exactly like I used to). All we do when we solve the problem is reward the bad behaviour of the complaint or problem by solving for them. We were Arse-Kissing. We were responding too gently – we were not allowing any ownership or accountability.

The other extreme is what we called Arse-Kicking – the manager who responds with an aggressive approach to an issue. There is no concern or respect when an issue is raised, it is punished with an approach that feels like a kick up the arse. The manager would tell the person they are stupid and should have resolved it already. They would then tell the employee what to do and hurry the heck up!

In both instances we could take a middle road between being the Arse-Kissing Manager and the Arse-Kicking Manager by being the Asking Leader. Before getting to the questions though, you will start the discussion with a statement: 'This is not good enough.'

We could then accept the issue and respond with some questions:

- 'Why is that a problem?'
- 'What impacts is it creating?'
- 'If you did fix it, how would we know?'
- 'What do you think you should do about it?'
- 'When will you have that done by?'

It may be that they are not achieving their goals, or it may be that they are just bad company around the workplace. It may be something quite serious such as a breach of privacy of company IP or even inappropriate behaviour around the water cooler. You are the CEO and it is your duty to state the situation clearly. There is no question in that statement. You didn't say, 'Do you agree that you have behaved badly at the water cooler?' That has already been resolved and clearly stated.

Your soonest opportunity for a question is immediately after the statement of error, 'What are you going to do about it?'

Doing nothing about it is not an option. 'When is that going to be done by?' 'How will I know the behaviour has changed?' 'We will meet again in x weeks to review your response.'

As ever, the Asking Leader has to have supreme self-discipline. We have to keep our emotions tightly bottled up in an imaginary jar in the back of our minds. We have to be simple, factual and on message. The Asking Leader is there to hear the plan to resolve the situation – that is all.

Eventually, your miscreant employee will go.

Another of my old farm managers used to say, 'I have never sacked anyone, but I have made a lot go.' He used to give them a string of really bad jobs and wait for them to tell him that he could 'stick the job up his arse'. The wily old bastard would then look disappointed and say, 'Geez mate, I'll miss ya. Keep in touch'. He would then 'phone the office and ask for the pay to be made up quick smart. He didn't want them changing their mind.

Needless to say, he wasn't much on exit interviews.

6. Exit Interview

There are a couple of purposes of an exit interview.

1. Find out what you can about the company and their thoughts
2. Make sure they leave with a good impression – even if they have been fired.

Just the process of asking questions will normally placate even the most annoyed of employees. They will often unload some spite and then it is done. It is out and gone. They can feel better for having said it.

The employees that are leaving to join another organisation can also be a bit spiteful. However, they will give you some insights that you may not be aware of and they will leave knowing that you are concerned for them.

Quite often an exit interview will allow you to keep a relationship with that person as they move on up the ladder in their career. From my own experience, I can say that I am proud of some of the young people who worked for me and then went on to bigger and better things. In fact, it still gives me a thrill to think of them and their success.

7. The Asking Leader makes for a great manager

Go back and have another look at the Herzberg table.

This HR process of the Asking Leader is about achieving those big and amorphous headings on the right-hand side of the table. They were:

- achievement
- recognition
- the work itself
- responsibility
- advancement
- growth.

Design a job description that encourages those critical aspects of an employee's life in your company. Have the curiosity and discipline to be the Asking Leader who creates that culture. Encourage the achievement, recognise it and celebrate it. Encourage your people to grow and learn, recognise the changes and advancements.

We all came to the role of CEO from another path. You never start as a CEO; you start as a specialist in something else. It might have been as a labourer or an engineer. Wherever you have come from, you are now not that labourer or engineer. You are now a manager of people. If you can be a good manager of people, you can be a great CEO.

Rate yourself out of 10:

- How effective and useful are your job descriptions?
- When doing interviews, how well do you look for evidence?
- How much more is your on boarding/introduction/induction than safety and compliance?
- How well do you review and discuss performance in terms of purpose, goals and strengths?
- How effective is your performance management process?
- How much value do you get from your exit interviews?

Sales

When anyone looks at the profit and loss statement, the easiest thing to understand is sales. You can quickly unpack the sales figures to year-on-year, monthly trends, percentage changes and more. It can be broken down into divisions and categories.

In my experience, not enough CEOs know about sales. Many can't differentiate between sales and marketing, and those that can, often can't get the two divisions to work together.

We now know that sales is not about telling. It is about asking.

"I don't have time to see any crazy salesman; I have a battle to fight."

Figure 3

The sales process has developed over the years. I reckon there are about four levels of sales:

1. We all know the Amway approach which is a **numbers** game. As they would say, 'Some will, some won't. So what? Let's get on with it.' The numbers game works well when there is a low level of personal touch.

2. The next level of sales came with a name: **relationship** sales. The banks really fell for this one when account managers became 'Relationship Managers'. The strong aspect of the relationship sale is often the value statement. 'My clients deal with me because …' The relationship manager has worked very hard to position their product accurately. They have done this by developing a deep connection with their clients. The idea is that, 'we will only do business with someone we like'. I don't believe the relationship sales approach is over. It is still very successful. It certainly works better than the numbers game.

3. The third level of selling is more of the **ASQ** model. If we ask the right series of questions, we will understand the buying criteria. We can then tailor a proposal that matches the criteria. This third level is more of a challenge to each other than a relationship. 'Let's show each other that we understand and then we will do business.'

4. The top level of sales is when they come to you. You are the **authority** on the subject. You have demonstrated that you already know what is happening and you are their solution. This level of sales is often aspired to but rarely achieved. However, if you can make it, price is not much of an issue anymore.

My first sales role was selling farm machinery for one of my family's companies. The total extent of the sales training I received from the company run by my uncle was a cassette recording of Zig Ziglar.

I would drive around the bush in my old ute and listen to Zig tell me that I needed:

'A check-up from the neck up'
'To eliminate the stinkin' thinkin''
'To avoid hardening of the attitudes'

Old Zig is still alive and well. Born in 1926, he has now gone through 90. What he taught me to do was be resilient. Never give up. In my parlance, it was to open that next gate and speak to that next farmer. He taught me to set goals and go after them.

I worked out that if I opened more gates and spoke to more farmers, I would get more sales. It was merely a function of numbers. I tracked the number of gates I had opened and compared that to sales and developed a ratio of gates to sales. Then I set a target to lower the ratio. Then I started to evaluate the average sale figure. I overlayed the sale size to the ratio. I found this all very motivating.

I was in level one sales mode. Amway – 'Some will, some won't; so what, get on with it.'

I had no practiced narrative on the values of our company, no simple pathway to a sale. I would just open the gate. Then my uncle employed a new salesman to work with me.

Didn't I get an eye-opener! This bloke came into the office like a whirlwind and tore me apart. He knew how to sell. He was a pressure salesman. Today, he would be called a 'Lone Wolf' salesman. He nearly threatened the customers, but he was successful.

Tractors and headers (harvesters) flew out the door. It was very exciting. It took a year or two for my uncle to discover that he had not maintained our margins. My uncle too was excited and beguiled by the whirlwind. I took some solace in that realisation, but the excitement of the new salesman still left me with that hollow feeling all salespeople know – I had been smashed by a pro.

I haven't looked at Zig for a while, but the idea of sales motivation is a long way from the current sophistication of the sales process. The current direction is more accurate through its focus on inquiry and challenge. There is sophistication in coming to a sale through a shared understanding of each other's needs.

What are the Impacts of Sales?

Let's not labour the point. Sales drive the businesses we are all in. I have been in quasi-government businesses that supply research and development services to agriculture and the government. These businesses did not think they had a sales issue. Every sale we got, in the form of a contract, lowered our administration costs, improved our buying power and raised our stakes in the eyes of our stakeholders.

I have advised CEOs with businesses that are collapsing in front of my eyes. The CEO wanted to focus on improving the efficiency of their factory. It takes a lot of discussion for them to realise that every sale did the following:

- lowered their marginal cost of production
- improved the efficiency of their factory more than the shiny new gadgets they wanted to buy
- lowered stock levels through better sales forecasting and production scheduling.

The easy way to increase sales is to drop the price. Heck, it works. But … dropping the price may mean dropping your margin. We have all seen seemingly successful sales systems that actually made less money after they are implemented. Sales is only the top number. Inherent in sales are the margins.

The only downside to improving sales is the risk of over-promising and under-delivering. In the professional services game of selling the time of highly skilled people (such as lawyers, accountants, engineers, surveyors, construction, prostitution, public relations, and so on), you have a choice to either:

1. backfill: grab a new shiny contract without having the staff to deliver on the promise or,
2. front-load: build-up the staff numbers before winning the contract.

The next risk of sales is the contingent risk of timing. I have seen many construction jobs sold to discover that the project is delayed. The construction company then has two problems:

1. enforced holidays: brought about by a hole in the program where that big job was going to be
2. overtime Paradise: an overlap which requires having to outsource to a competitor to meet the contract.

Certainly, the impacts of sales are usually positive. However, they can present deeper management challenges that CEOs are all too aware of.

What would a Successful sales system look like?

We would know if our sales system was working if:

- sales go up
- margins are maintained or grow
- marginal costs of production are lowered
- there is improved efficiency and timing of production
- there are lower administration costs and overheads
- costs of each sale are lowered
- the risks of over-promising and under-delivering are managed.

There are many more success measures. What are yours? www.askingleader.com.

What's the Plan?

Achieving a successful sales system is understanding that first and foremost, sales are a process. To create a successful system for sales, there must be a process.

Every company should have a sales process.

Big or small, fat or thin. Do not let yourselves say 'oh yeah, but we're different.' In business- to-consumer, business-to-business, and even the soulless internet sales where no people are involved, sales is a process.

You and your sales team should have an agreed way to represent your brand, manage the conversations, create the successes and measure them.

Secondly, the sales process needs to be continually refined. Regular intervals of practice and review.

Don't tell, ASQ.

If you stand in front of a sales prospect and tell them all about your product, explain why you think it is good for them, explain the value proposition and then ask, 'Do you wanna buy it?' you have committed the cardinal sin of ASQ.

You have asked a closed question.

The answer can be 'No.' You need to ask questions so that the answer is 'Yes'.

The ASQ sales system in action

One of my clients was overly dependent on one company for work. He supplies professional services to infrastructure developers. He was extremely concerned that he needed that company to give him their next contract. He was totally exasperated with the stress of needing that next contract from his main customer. I had never seen him like this. His exasperation was deep and was affecting his health.

He told me that he, 'wants to give it all up! Go back to just me out in the field doing what I loved!' He had had a gutful of working for big companies and employing people.

My first task was to get his head back in the game. We had a brutal conversation about resilience. 'When the going gets tough, the tough get going.' 'I didn't know you are a quitter.' And more.

Then we discussed how he could be sure he could win that contract.

We went back to our training from Robyn Haydon and her book, *Winning Again*

. We decided that we wouldn't directly address the new contract. We would directly address the completion of the existing contract. Our strategy was to make sure the customer was happy with my client's current performance. We wanted to remind them that they were happy by asking them. We didn't want to tell them that they were happy with his delivery. We wanted them to tell us. We wanted to do that by Asking a Designed Series of Questions – ASQ.

We set up an 'End of Contract Review' meeting with the two main advisors in the company. As an Asking Leader, we **designed a series of questions** and we walked the customer through them.

The two officials were a bit surprised at the process. It had never been done to them before. They weren't uncomfortable, just a bit amused.

We asked:

1. How did we communicate with you?
   - Did it meet your needs?
   - How can we improve our communication?
   - How did our team interact with your team.?
2. Did our report properly meet the technical and compliance aspects of your needs?
   - Where can we improve in that area?

- What did we do well that we should continue to develop?

3. Would you recommend us as professionals in this field?

   When we asked the final question, the two officials looked at each other and gave a little smile.

   'Yes', they said.

   A couple of weeks later, without completing the final tender documents, my client was awarded the next contract. That contract alone grew his business by twenty per cent. All of his anxiety and worry flew out the window. He rang me to celebrate. I too was thrilled. It was a wonderful moment in both our careers.

   Several months later he won an award for being the best in his profession in NSW. He has now been approached by several other large-scale infrastructure companies to work with them. My client has moved from the relationship sale to the ASQ sales level. He is now becoming an authority in his field.

   For me, as his business coach, the whole exercise was a thrill. That is why I coach.

An easy way to apply the ASQ model

I just love the simplicity of Greg Donlan's BANTER. He is a great sales trainer who focuses on developing a sales process with his clients. Greg says rather than tell, ask. The BANTER is just one example of the series of questions to ask. The BANTER series of questions is a simple acronym that is easy to remember and easy to apply.

When I get stuck in nearly any situation, I defer to BANTER:

1. **Budget**

   1.1 How much are you expecting to spend?

    1.2   How does your budgeting work for this type of purchase?

2. **Authority**

    2.1   How does the decision process work?

    2.2   Who makes it?

    2.3   A board, you, the line manager?

    2.4   What do they need to help make a decision?

3. **Needs**: what do you need or expect from the:

    3.1   Product

    3.2   Service

    3.3   Supplier?

4. **Timing**

    4.1   When? How soon?

    4.2   Over what period?

    4.3   Are their milestones along the way?

5. **Experiences**

    5.1   How have you done this in the past?

    5.2   What went well?

    5.3   What could have been better?

    5.4   How does that inform this decision?

6. **Re-book (**I love this one)

    6.1   When can I come back and develop this solution further?

    6.2   You said you have to make a decision in a month, let's come back next Monday and I will see if I can prepare something that meets your needs.

    6.3   In the meantime, can you find out about the x, y and z that we are not yet sure on? Challenge the customer to do some homework.

When my clients are in doubt, if they can only ask the **Needs** and **Experiences** questions, they will be a long way to developing a winning relationship with that client.

Greg is teaching 'discovery'. He is saying that the sales team needs to take the time to discover the client's real needs and experiences so that they can then package the subsequent proposal to meet those needs.

Once the sales team gets past that discovery stage then the next stages of any program are more aligned with the Challenger sales processes. Again, the Challenger process is about asking questions. The idea is that customers want to talk about their business and not your solution. If the sales team can listen thoroughly then they will let the customer tell them the solution they need. If the sales team have the **self-discipline to be sufficiently curious** to find the customer's real needs, they will close more sales.

The price of the solution is then a secondary issue. The primary issue of the solution itself gets you most of the way over the line.

This is a sure way to protect your margins.

What comes after BANTER?

I use BANTER as the basis of nearly any sales situation. I use it as a basis of a more targeted inquiry that suits each particular circumstance. The first one I developed was for consulting clients. I called it 'Discover DEAD'. Notwithstanding the macabre title, the acronym is an easy way for me to remember the steps of my process. The process begins with BANTER and ends with a completed report for the client:

- **Discover** stage is the discovery process that is BANTER. The purpose is to find out what the client really wants.

- **D**efine is to confirm that you have heard what they wanted and come back with a few proposals that we can work on with the client. Continue to reflect on the stated need of the client and determine the pathway to meet the need.
- **E**ngage is to conclude the development of the proposal into an agreement. Set the timelines and deliverables to meet the timing needs stated in the BANTER discovery.
- **A**ssess the performance of the agreement along the way. Maybe monthly, or whatever the client prefers. Set nice tidy timelines that the client can anticipate. Find out if anything has changed during the period and if the goalposts have moved – they often do. Find out if there are any other tasks that need to be added to complete the original task. Find out what the client is anticipating in the next phase after this task has been completed.
- **D**eliver the final report. Compare the report against the objectives. Ask for feedback in a formal meeting that covers off all aspects of your delivery. Begin to discover and define any other work they may have coming.

The Assess and Deliver stages are the stages that determine your future with the client. If you know they have more work coming, then asking these questions along the journey will help you stay on the inside track to get the next job.

On-Line Sales

On-line sales aren't so different.

Several of my clients are in the on-line arena of business. They all talk about it with the religious fervour of the recently converted. If one more person tells me that Uber doesn't own a car and Airbnb doesn't own any property I will scream and commit a violent act. Personally, I don't think that the on-line business world is that different from every other business.

All businesses have to identify demand and meet it at a competitive price. They have to develop people and systems to achieve that. The big successful companies have been able to aggregate enormous volumes of demand and match it with supply that was usually thought unavailable – such as a car in someone's garage or a spare bedroom in someone's house.

Brilliant. But the business principles still apply.

The CEO of the on-line business has to ASQ just like any other CEO The sales side of the on-line business is just the same. The ASQ CEO will be asking questions in the same way of the sales team as in any other business.

However, the on-line business can be an authority. The on-line business can assume the top level of sales by establishing credibility that only comes from offering products and services that are finely tuned to the needs of their customers.

Let's go back to BANTER.

The on-line business already knows the **needs** and **experiences** of the customers.

They know **Budget**. They know that if you are clicking on their site, you have the **authority** to make that decision.

They know how to **re-book** with you because they just harvested all of your contact details (and your birthday so they can send you an annoying birthday email).

But they didn't apparently ask one question. How can that be?

Actually, they did ASQ. They asked those questions by aggregating vast amounts of data. They use sophisticated analytics to create your profile so that they become the authority. The technology is all very impressive, but simple business principles still work.

No matter the product or the technology used to sell it, moving through the sales stages of the numbers game, the relationship sale to the ASQ sales approach is the only pathway to the aspiration of becoming the authority.

Accountability – the Asking Leader makes sense of sales

Every sales team knows that the accountability of sales is in the metrics. The measurement of the sales team is more than simply counting the money in the till. The measurement of sales is always in the numbers. Some of my clients get seriously excited by these numbers! The on-line sales analytics are so accurate that there is no room for error. The big construction companies know the cost of every tender. All will know their conversion rates and their expenditure to sales ratios. They will see the trends and be able to forecast the changes.

Asking Leaders will have a system of sales metrics that is accessible, instant and understandable. You will ensure the information is at the fingertips of all who can contribute. You will want them to understand the issues and want to harvest their contribution.

However, the discipline to look at the numbers and discuss them so the sales team can develop insights and offer solutions is still a critical step of the Asking Leader.

This will:

- grow your sales
- maintain your margins

- lower your marginal costs of production
- improve your efficiency and timing of production
- lower your administration costs and overheads
- manage the risk of over-promising and under-delivering.

What works in your organisation? What have you been working on? www.askingleader.com

Marketing

'I know that half of my marketing budget is wasted.
I just don't know which half.'
Did you say that?

What's the Issue about Marketing?

The CEOs who see marketing clearly understand that the purpose of the marketing department is to create qualified inquiries. It is that **simple**. Marketing is to create qualified inquiries for the sales team to convert to dollars.

Other CEOs see marketing as **complex**. Marketing is to express their brand values and extol the wonders of their magnificent product or service. Done well, it positions the company favourably in the marketplace, explains the value proposition and overcomes our customer's need to focus on the price. Today, it also engages social media by improving the number of 'likes'.

In my experience of sitting with many CEOs, the role of sales and marketing are inextricably linked. There are many configurations but, in every instance, the role of the CEO is to be the CEO. I have seen:

- larger companies with separate departments of sales and marketing both of whom report to the CEO and are members of the Senior Leadership Team
- larger companies with separate departments of sales and marketing which both report to the Senior Leadership Team through a Sales and Marketing Director
- smaller companies which have in-house sales and marketing teams
- smaller companies which outsource the marketing role but have kept the sales role in-house
- smaller family-styled companies where the CEO is also the sales and marketing manager. This requires the CEO to 'change hats'. They must think like a CEO, and then think separately like the sales/marketing manager. Then they must think like a CEO again. They must measure themselves with dry-eyed analytics rather than back their own judgement and not know which half of their marketing budget is wasted.

There is a famous old statement from an American executive who said, 'I know that half of what I spend on advertising is wasted. I just don't know which half'.

Today, you know which half. The metrics in sales are now so thorough that every dollar spent can be interrogated for its efficacy. The analytics give automated reports that are accurate to the second. Even my LinkedIn site tells me how popular I am (not)! (However, it does annoy me when it tells everyone it is my birthday!)

The CEO must design the series of questions that create the success the company needs.

What are the Impacts of the marketing issues?

The CEOs who see marketing as complex are right – if they are the marketing manager. If they are the CEO, then they are complicating the marketing role in their own heads and if they're any good as Asking Leader CEOs, they are already busy leading higher-level challenges.

From the perspective of the CEO, there are four main impacts of a successful or unsuccessful marketing team:

1. Simplicity
    1.1 CEOs tend to believe they have some ideas about marketing, so they enter the debate and (often) bugger it up. Their preference for this channel or that, this message or that, is where the trouble begins.
2. Unity
    3.1 The sales and marketing teams are often two riders on the same horse, facing in different directions. No wonder the horse is confused.
    2.2 The connection across the business into production or service delivery creates both oversupplies and undersupplies.
3. Value
    3.1 We can know which half of our marketing budget it wasted. Particularly in today's world of digital metrics and Customer Relationship Software (CRM) products.
4. Opportunity
    4.1 If we get this right, we can succeed:
    - Feel good about what it is that we do
    - Be rewarded with recognition and financially.

The Asking Leader CEO needs to have the marketing department focus on qualified leads.

The catch is the word 'qualified'.

The half of our spending on marketing that is wasted is spent on leads that are not our potential or preferred customers. Now we know which half of our marketing budget is wasted.

The second issue with marketing is that the sales department are useless. Every marketing department the world over, thinks the sales department are incompetent fools who couldn't sell ice cream to children on a hot Sunday at the beach.

Each marketing department creates enormous numbers of fantastic leads and they go nowhere! 'What can we do? We do our best work and they just lose them! They are bunch of over-indulged show ponies!' And worse … Much worse!'

The third issue is the poor bastards in production. Both the sales and marketing teams just go to lunches, take boxes at the rugby and spend the rest of the day brushing their hair. The poor mob in production are (apparently) working tirelessly and quietly while stocks on hand go through the roof and they get orders they can't fill that are needed to be filled tomorrow.

If you are a service company, the marketing team creates work when we already have too much, and they do bugger all when we are quiet. How can we plan for that?

There's a fourth and final issue. Finance. The finance team think marketing is a black hole of unaccountability. Finance will say that, 'We would get better value from our marketing expenditure if we didn't spend it all!'

'The whole marketing team are a bunch of arty-farty types who think they have an innate understanding of the human psyche! To these people, money is not an issue.' 'They're like reindeer – we call them Donna, Blitzen, Dancer and Prancer. The one who drinks too much is called Rudolph!'

The best analogy I have heard on marketing came from a big brand wine company that spent heavily on marketing – particularly sponsorships in various sports. The finance guy said: 'We would lose less money on that brand if we just gave the wine away.'

What is a successful marketing plan?

If we had a good marketing plan how would we know? What does success mean in marketing?

1. Simplicity and value: how would our Asking Leader CEO know if we were running a successful marketing program?
   - Number of qualified leads going into the sales team
   - Conversions of those leads by the sales team
   - Cost per qualified lead
   - Cost per converted sale.
2. Unity: is the business working together?
   - An across the business understanding that a qualified lead aligns with the overall purpose of the business and values of the team
   - Planning of the balance between our capacity to supply and sales. Do we have the:
     - resources
     - time
     - skills … and more.
3. Opportunity: do we all understand the impacts of success?

The Asking Leader's Plan

Firstly, the Asking Leader must design a job description that keeps the role out of the CEOs office. When designing the role of the marketing manager, the goals must be very clear:

1. Create qualified leads that convert to sales
2. Lower the cost of the qualified leads and converted sales
3. Engage across the business to ensure the balance of sales and supply.

Secondly, the CEO must ensure the marketing team has a suitable plan to meet the outcomes. They must design the plan and present it to the CEO. As with all plans, there must be clearly measurable outcomes, milestones and accountabilities.

The Asking Leader business owner without the resources for a marketing department must actively think like a marketing manager with those goals. The business owner will get advice, employ consultants and build a plan. Then, become the Asking Leader CEO again and review it without too much empathy for the poor person who wrote the plan – themselves.

Finally, the CEO must ensure the Senior Leadership Team understands the marketing plan and agrees to its strategies. The sales, finance, production, and service delivery teams understand the alignment with the overall purpose, goals and values of the company.

How will we know we have been successful? How can we be Accountable?

There are many marketing measures. They are intricate and beguiling. Many CEOs fall into the trance of the psychobabble that comes from the marketing department.

The Asking Leader CEO will have the self-discipline to remain above the conversation of the colour of the logo ('cerise will never work – too pink! I do like the lavender colour') and focus on the big numbers. The Asking Leader will ensure that marketing is an integral and critical part of our business by engaging the Senior Leadership Team in the connectivity of marketing and sales across the whole business.

The Asking Leader CEO will know which half of the marketing budget is wasted.

Board and Senior Leadership Team

Herding the top cats.

The CEO can **lead** the development of a **shared protocol of success**. Again, as ever, this can be done by asking. Asking in a way that creates accountability and success. Specifically, this book is about CEO leadership. Let's consider that through the prism of the Asking Leader.

It always sounds like a contradiction of terms. How can you lead by asking questions?

'It doesn't sound like leadership to me. It sounds like 'followship'.

Let's think back to the great leaders of our recent times. Who are they for you?

For me, I am a paid-up member of the Nelson Mandela Fan Club. Mandela showed incredible forgiveness when he left Robbin Island after being incarcerated for 27 years. He forgave his captors. After 27 years of brutality and deprivation he had the humility and foresight to forgive his Apartheid captors. Simultaneously, he neutered his enemies and shone a light for his people to follow.

He had the insight to know that responding with violence and civil disobedience was going to play into the hands of his enemy. He surprised them with his passivity.

Furthermore, he knew that his own people were tired of the treadmill they had worn thin over the past 27 years. He was aware of the vocal minority within the African National Congress who wanted to confront the Apartheid government with fear and fire, but he was also aware of the quiet majority who wanted to be shown another path.

Mandela tapped that sentiment and spoke with them about how that could work. He then showed them the pathway.

That is 'followship'.

Think also about John Howard. Our conservative Prime Minister with views that could be described as old-fashioned. His upbringing and heritage were suburban Australian with a splashback of old England. His middle name is Winston.

When Martin Bryant did the unspeakable at Port Arthur in Tasmania, John Howard did the unspeakable to his conservative constituents. He took our guns.

That dreadful act of cowardice from Martin Bryant found a remarkable act of courage from John Howard. We had to hand in our guns – myself included. We had to get gun licences and prove that we could be safe with them. Australia led the world in gun reform and is now the shining light for our American cousins to follow – and they never will.

We weren't too happy about handing in our guns, but we did it anyway. A few farmers that I knew went to the trouble of hiding their guns, but most were handed in. We liked the idea of owning a semi-automatic weapon but we didn't really need one – and now we don't miss them at all. One fellow I knew hid his guns and wore a T-shirt emblazoned with, 'They can have my guns when they take them from my cold dead hands'. He wasn't the brightest spark in the campfire, and I am pretty sure the police knew where to find his guns.

Now we are proud of what John Howard did. We are proud of where Australia stands against the daily horror of the USA.

John Howard did not display 'followship' that day. That was leadership. He took an unimaginable risk and it paid off.

Others who have followed Howard have tried to emulate his leadership. Recently, Mike Baird as Premier of NSW, banned the greyhound racing industry. There had been shameful cruelty in that industry as many dogs had been inhumanely slaughtered. However, Baird got it wrong. He took the risk and he didn't get Howard's reward. He banned the greyhound racing in NSW and then lost the ensuing backlash.

Finally, let's consider Elon Musk. His values align with the populace and he is making it work. Every time he speaks, he is lauded as a genius because he has been able to do what so many around the world want done. He has managed to disrupt the automobile industry and break through the oil industry's dominance of powering cars.

In so doing, he has developed an enormous team of motivated engineers to deliver 'our' dream. He has made engineering and science sexy. However, we have all read that he can be 'difficult' to work for.

Becoming an Asking Leader CEO

CEOs can storm up to the lectern at the Annual Company meetings and give grand visions, make statements of their own successes and purport to inspire the proletariat and shareholders with their wisdom and insight. Then, with some theatre, they descend from the stage and are warmly slapped on the back by the lesser mortals. Hail-fellow-well-met.

That's terrific. But what then? How does the wildly popular, brilliant and insightful, kind and magnanimous CEO transform his words into actions that create the changes they have promised.

Enter stage right, with no fanfare and only little applause, the Asking Leader.

After the grand speeches and glossy reports in the annual statements, the two direct pathways of influence for the Asking Leader is the Board of Directors and the Senior Leadership Team. The Asking Leader must manage both up and down. In both instances the process for the Asking Leader is the same.

As ever in this book of the Asking Leader, it is to plan for and ask a series of questions that are designed to create a **shared protocol of success**.

1. Establish the purpose of both the Board of Directors and the Senior Leadership Team:
   1.1 Why are we here?
   1.2 What are our personal expectations?
   1.3 What are our organisational expectations?
2. Establish the measures of success. Goals or objectives:
   2.1 What are we trying to achieve?
   2.2 What are each of our personal needs in the SLT?
3. Encourage behaviours:
   3.1 How do we deal with each other?
   3.2 Which behaviours are preferred?
   3.3 Which are discouraged?
   3.4 How do we make decisions?
4. Systems:
   How do we keep minutes?
   How do we present ideas?
   How do we report against the goals?

5. Cadence:

   How much time should meetings take?

   How often is often enough to meet?

6. Accountability:

   How do we keep each other accountable?

   How do we recognise achievement?

   How do we address the targets that were missed?

7. Review (I use POBSCAR another silly acronym that helps me remember the protocol):

   Purpose

   Objectives

   Behaviours

   Systems

   Cadence

   Accountability

   Review – yes, even the review of the review:

   - How did this review go?
   - Did it take our shared protocol of success up to another level?
   - Is that high enough?
   - What should we look for in the next review?

The Asking Leader CEO is the link between them all. The Asking Leader is not the 'doer' who answers every inquiry with an answer.

The Asking Leader answers with questions that develop engagement, accountability and success.

The board appoint the CEO and then set strategy, monitor performance, ensure compliance, and manage risk. Further, the board must ensure the company will meet community expectations and the expectations of the shareholders.

That's a lot going on.

The Senior Leadership Team must deliver the strategy to hundreds of customers, employees and suppliers.

That too is a lot going on.

The challenge for the CEO in this instance is the loneliness. The CEO is the centre point of much pressure. To achieve this incredible balancing act, I think it is best that the CEO is not a member of either the Board or the Senior Leadership Team. The CEO is certainly a participant, but not a member.

The Boardroom

In the boardroom, the CEO is like a guest. The CEO appreciates the guidance of the board by presenting ideas for them to support. A good board will only have one of three replies:

1. Yes, we agree with your proposal
2. No, we don't agree with your proposal
3. We need more information.

A good CEO will score with lots of 1s and no 2s. A few 3s are allowed, if they are temporary and soon become a 1. To achieve the low scores, the CEO's presentations must align very closely with the clear requirements of the board. The proposal should:

1. Ask that the outcome of the proposal is in **alignment** with the:
   - company's purpose
   - strategic plan.
2. Show that the resources required:
   - Are available or accessible
   - Will provide a suitable return.
3. Have a simple and effective accountability with:
   - Milestones
   - Measures.

The minutes, or records of the board meetings are often open to interpretation (just like every piece of law ever written!) The CEO can often misunderstand the conclusions of the board meeting. The Chairman has two duties here:

1. Ensure the minutes are specific and accurately reflect the decision of the board.
2. Be the only source of interpretation between the board and the CEO, between meetings;
   2.1 Directors should not give the CEO guidance on the decisions of the board.

The Senior Leadership Team

The Senior Leadership Team is the interface between the CEO and the people who must deliver the decisions of the board. The Asking Leader will be empowering it to create the delivery.

This is different to how I see most CEOs working. Most believe it is their responsibility to ensure delivery. If they were the great manager with all the right answers, that would be true. But they are the leader, the Asking Leader.

The great CEO with all the right questions will empower and monitor the Senior Leadership Team to deliver. The CEO is separate. In the boardroom, the CEO is the guest. In the Senior Leadership Team, the CEO is the convenor.

However, Senior Leadership Teams often fail to work together. Many come together every month to represent their own silos:

- The representative of production will be there to complain that the customer team are not getting the orders in on time
- The customer team will complain that they have been unsuccessful because the HR team are not selecting the right people
- The HR team will complain that the finance team are not giving them enough money to employ the right people
- And the Finance team will blame everyone for underperforming.

This is not the Senior Leadership Team; it is the Silos of Blame. The SOB. And it is a son-of-a-bitch to run. The SOB meeting is about whingeing and arse-covering. All the problems are put to the CEO with the question – 'What are you going to do about it?' The CEO manager with all the answers will provide answers. 'You do this, I'll do that. We'll get through it somehow.'

The Asking Leader CEO has created a Senior Leadership Team to be a team! They are not there to represent their silos and blame each other. It is the opposite – they participate in the team because they want to work together to meet the objectives of the company. The Asking Leader CEO will lead the leaders. You guessed it, with questions – with a designed series of questions that the Senior Leadership Team become comfortable with.

And you know it, those questions create the engagement and accountability.

What do you have in your company? A SLT or a SOB?

Can you create a SLT? Tell us about your experiences at www. askingleader.com/SLT

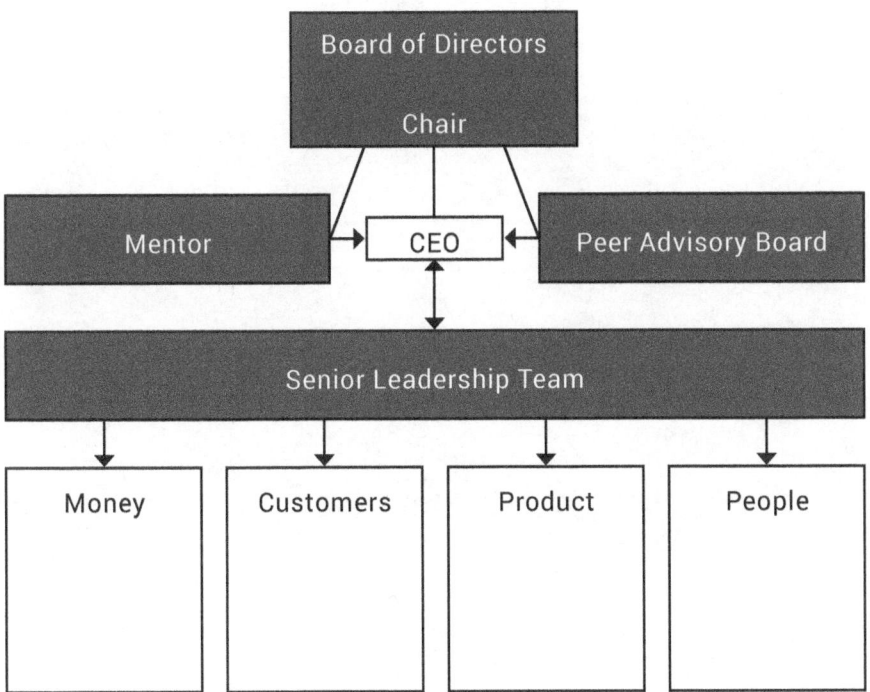

Strategy — the Ultimate Asking Leader Challenge

I have left strategic planning for the last chapter in this book, because it is the ultimate challenge of the Asking Leader.

This chapter will not give you my preferred strategic planning process. I don't have one. This chapter does not have a natty little acronym.

I will encourage you as the Asking Leader to think above the planning process so that you consider a higher-level framework for your planning.

If you can succeed in strategic planning, you are good.

Damned good!

The positive impacts of strategic planning

Strategic planning is a high-risk activity. It can work out well.

1. **Financial success**

   Good strategic planning can do wonders. It can reverse a downtrend, expand a successful pathway, and identify new subpathways that complement the existing business. Strategic planning can create the **financial** success that your company has dreamed was possible.

2. **Cultural success**

   The most important impact of good strategic planning is **unity**. CEOs, Boards of Directors and the Senior Leadership Teams need to recognise the positive impact of good planning on the **culture** and attitude of the whole company.

3. **Good investment**

   Strategic planning can be a good investment. Accepting that strategic planning is expensive and time-consuming means that the organisation must be committed to getting **value** from that time and money.

   What else do you think is an opportunity in your strategic planning?

Challenges in strategic planning

Of course, the **flipside** is true.

Bad strategic planning can be a **financial disaster**. Investments can be made that will not work. Precious retained earnings and cash can be squandered. We can all think of examples where a company has zigged when it should have zagged. Too often, the cause of the poor choices has been a dominant player in the room. One person's idea of the future takes control – no matter the advice to the contrary. The loudest person in the room—often with the cheque book—has an idea that we are going to stop what we are doing and do something shiny and new.

I have heard these business leaders called 'squirrels'. They chase the next shiny object they find and then they forget about it because they have found another one.

One of my clients used to bring a 'new idea' to our Peer Advisory Board every three or four months. He had a very profitable business that no longer excited him. His business had not yet reached even a small proportion of its potential. Yet he would let his mind drift to the next idea that popped up in front of him.

Often, he would want to risk the whole company on the new shiny object. To us, he seemed to be hell-bent on self-destruction. Every time, without fail, our Peer Advisory Board would give him the same message, 'don't be stupid!'

If he had presented those ideas to his own team, they would have been duty-bound to agree with him. In his company, he was the strongest person in the room. If he had made that decision at that level, they would have unwillingly gone along with the strategy.

Thanks to his peers, he still has a wonderful and growing business.

The **cultural risks** of strategic planning are potentially as damaging as the financial risks.

They are:

- a disengaged workforce
- a Senior Leadership Team that has reverted to its old habits of the Silos of Blame
- a Board of Directors that want your scalp.

Have you ever been into a company and you see their strategic plan posted up on the wall? 'We will blah blah blah...'

Take the time to ask someone in the company about the plan. I did it once and the reply was, 'Oh that! It's something management do. Nothing to do with us mate.'

Finally, the cost of the plan. Simply, you can spend big money and get **no value**.

What else do you think is a risk in your strategic planning:

1. The role of directors

As Chairman of the Board, I would notice that our **Directors** would get very excited about strategic planning. They would sit forward in their seats and gently scratch their chins in a vain effort to hide their excitement. Strategic planning is one of the reasons people want to be a Director. Strategic planning is their chance to display their great insight and wisdom.

I often ask Directors why they have been appointed to the board. They will reply that it is because of their strategic perspective, their vast experience in the industry, or their external view. While that may be partly true, they never mention that the real reason they have been appointed has less to do with their experience or perspective than the fact that the board thinks that their appointment will attract capital or appeal to shareholders' needs.

The Directors know they should do all that compliance stuff, risk management, measuring and monitoring. They sit there for months going through the agony of the arse-covering, so they can have the privilege of the exciting stuff. In fact, they only like two things: strategic planning and appointing the CEO.

Oh, the other thing that Directors love to do, is meddle. We have all seen Directors argue over the font in the annual report. The colour of the new product. The battery size in the new version.

The military say that the 'Generals' will take minutes to approve the purchase of hardware worth millions, and then spend the rest of the day arguing over the new design of the brass buttons on the parade uniforms.

Sometimes, the Directors get to meddle in the strategic planning exercise. Who the facilitator should be, how often the meetings should be held, which venue (always exceedingly grand) and who the presenters should be. Sometimes, they think the presenters should be themselves.

2. The outcomes for management

If the CEO had a challenge getting a plan agreed upon, the next challenge of implementing it is frightening. The winners of the plan are strutting around with an unpleasant air of arrogance. The losers are being consoled as they run interference on every subsequent decision.

Management often cower in fear about the strategic plan. They meet in corridors and discuss the likely outcome of the plan – especially with those three new Directors! 'One is an engineer! Two of them think they are very clever – and they aren't'.

The uncertainty that comes from strategy is often a source of deep angst and instability in the Senior Leadership Team. Strategy is one of the company activities that cause the level of employee satisfaction and engagement to drop. Whole divisions can be scrapped. New directions can be created. Careers can be ruined by a flippant 'thought bubble' on a piece of butchers paper.

There are two times each year when they start looking on job websites – strategic planning time and the week after Christmas.

They know that **'Implementation Confusion'** is the phase that comes immediately after the plan is declared – and the directors have departed the grand venue in their business class cabins eating canapes and drinking decent wines. Management know there will be insufficient attention paid to the details. There will never be enough resources to achieve the grand plans. The fanciful time goals looked terrific when written in coloured markers on the whiteboard but are unachievable in the 'real world'.

Beyond the personal behaviour of the main players, the big challenge with strategic planning is **scope**. How big, how far, how long, just plain how, and what next. How do you put together such a plan?

3. How deep?

If you bring in a consultant, it will be big. Their report is sold by the kilogram. Thousands of pages convert directly to thousands of dollars. Perhaps hundreds of thousands of dollars. There will be pages of 'background' information that will show their depth of knowledge in your business. At the end of the report, there needs to be an outcome. What are we going to do? How deep does the research and backgrounding need to be to make that recommendation? Can we overcome the old 'paralysis by analysis'?

Some companies need depth and some companies need to be encouraged to think more widely.

Imagine running a strategic plan for a company of professionals – lawyers, accountants and engineers. These professions love depth but need width. They need to be challenged to think with less detail than their profession has trained them. Accuracy is paramount.

Then imagine running a strategic plan for a company of creatives – TV and movie production, advertising. They love width but need depth. Their creative mindset is trained to head off over the horizon without prompting. Details are for other people.

How deep should we go into the layers of the organisation? Who should be consulted? All consultants have been told that we can only talk to the board of directors and the CEO. Sometimes we are allowed access to senior management, but not the chap at the end of the corridor because he is on his way out. Rarely are we allowed a company-wide role.

Often, the subjects are market sensitive. Sometimes the plan is to float, or sell, or divest. That type of information would unsettle the horses. Sometimes the board is just plain secretive and will not share information.

4. How far?

How far beyond the existing business are we going to consider? According to Matthew Tice of Insurgence Pty Ltd, strategy needs to consider the scope of its thinking. He describes the need for strategy in an unstable environment. How far can the plan go to challenge deeply held limits to the company's capacity to think beyond the incremental improvements that most people expect?

How can the group consider innovative ideas that make them uncomfortable?

Simon Sinek, in his soon to be released book, *The Infinite Game,* talks of overcoming the limits of our thinking by thinking of business as 'infinite'. He prefers that we don't think so much about endpoint in business, but we think more about new opportunities. He says, "there are no winners and losers in an infinite game; there is only ahead and behind".

He reminds me of the football coach who says, 'focus on the components of our performance and the score will look after itself'. Sinek says we should plan to focus on building the capacity of the individuals rather than quarterly earnings. He says we should focus on longer-term relationships with customers rather than sales. In that, we will 'build stronger, more innovative, more inspiring organisations'.

5. How long?

The timeframe is always a challenge. Many companies struggle to think one-year ahead. All plans try to achieve a three-year horizon. Everyone thinks that five or ten years is mindless daydreaming. All consultants will try to get the organisation to think twenty-years ahead – just to achieve a five-year plan. We all know that asking a company to think five-years ahead will only achieve a one-year plan.

I had a client whom I was trying to convince to think twenty-years ahead. He runs a large farming estate that had been in the family for many hundreds of years. His answer was that he should think 150 years ahead. Given that the building we were sitting in was 200 years old and built by his great-great-uncle and the home in which he lives with his young family was last renovated in 1911, he described that his impact must be of a similar time frame. Notwithstanding the circumstances of agriculture at the time, this insightful young man wanted to accept a longer challenge. He was prepared to see past climate change, urbanisation, energy prices, artificial intelligence, and heaven-knows-what-else, to build a long-term plan.

Putting together a plan

After reading so many chapters of this book, you will know what to do.

Ask.

Even better, before you commence any activity you will ASQ. You will design a series of questions to **build the framework** of your strategic plan. The framework will be designed to manage the positive and negative impacts of the plan and create the outcomes the company needs. The Asking Leader does not need to build a process for strategic planning, the Asking Leader needs to be a level above the process.

You need to be designing the larger framework that manages the risks, creates the opportunities and delivers the outcomes. Your level of thinking imagines the planning process as only a part of the framework.

The Asking Leader will have no need to go into the planning phase with any preconceived outcomes. You will have the confidence in your Senior Leadership Team and your Board to create them for you. You will be subtle enough to guide the outcome with the right questions at the right time. You will ensure they 'own' the plan.

If you are to create a larger framework, which questions would you ask?

How would you understand the needs and experiences of the Board and the SLT:

1. How deep do they think the plan should be?
   The level of analysis
   Consultation within the business
   Consultation with stakeholders
2. How challenging in terms of the balance between business-as-usual (BAU) and transformation?
3. How far into the future should the plan consider? Or should it be infinite – as Simon Sinek suggests?
4. How do we resource the plan?
   4.1 How much should it cost?
       - Do we employ consultants?
       - Speakers, challengers?
       - Offsite venues?
5. Which planning process do they think best suits the needs?
6. What else can we do to ensure ownership and engagement?
7. When does the plan need to be completed?
8. How do we monitor and evaluate the plan?
9. How do we manage and resource the implementation phases?

What Next?

At the end of the planning phase, do you have a plan to manage the Implementation Confusion? Does the board have further roles and responsibilities within the plan to ensure its delivery? Has the

Senior Leadership Team united in its approach to the delivery? Do they understand their individual and collective roles?

Measuring success

For you as the CEO, the criteria of the strategic plan need to be clear. You will need to ensure the plan is financially successful, culturally positive and a good investment.

1. Create clear outcomes?
    1.1 Is the plan BAU with a ten per cent improvement in things?
    1.2 Is the plan a transformational approach with all new, singing and dancing gadgetry and whiz-bangery?
    1.3 Is it a balance of BAU with some transformational strategies that are of a manageable risk?
2. Suitable measures?
    2.1 Does the plan create real and measurable outcomes across more aspects of the business than finance?
    2.2 Does the plan set dates for the steps in the new pathway?
3. Possible?
    3.1 Does it have an achievable plan with the necessary resources:
        - People and their capacity
        - Finance for investment
        - Market need for the strategy
        - Competitive space.
    3.2 Is there an in-built review process?
        - Five yearly
        - Annually
        - Ninety days

- Monthly.

4. Commitment with passion.

    4.1 Do we have a measure of the feeling within the company about the new plan? Can we monitor that over time?

    4.2 Have all the players been engaged? Will they continue to be engaged?

5. What else?

    5.1 What else do you think is an important measure of success of your strategic plan?

Accountability of the plan

Asking Leaders knows their main role is to develop and maintain accountability. Many strategic plans are quickly forgotten when there is no in-built accountability. Forests have been sacrificed in the printing of strategic plans that were never implemented.

Every step of the Asking Leader is to encourage the teams to 'own' the strategy and the outcome. Every step is to create a culture of accountability that will become ingrained with time. The culture becomes the norm. When creating a strategic plan, the culture of accountability must be built-in.

As the fulcrum between the Board and the Senior Leadership Team, you need to ensure the ownership across the company that you have developed in the plan is balanced with accountability. It is not completely true that the CEO can hold the Board accountable. The CEO can help the board create the correct culture of accountability. When the board signs off the final version of the plan, the roles of the board should be clear. So too will be the accountability of the board.

Creating the culture can be as simple as asking for it.

1. Let's talk about accountability. What does that mean?
2. What would happen if we were better at holding ourselves accountable? How much will accountability affect the implementation of the plan?
3. What do we do now?
4. What should or could we do to hold each other accountable?
5. What are we going to do to hold each other accountable?
6. How will we measure that?

How are you going to have the self-discipline to ensure accountability?

By now, as an Asking Leader, you already know the answer.

Conclusion

I have had many CEOs think through this journey to become the Asking Leader. The rate of uptake varies:

1. some love it and pick it up quickly
2. most like it and pick it up in parts
3. and some don't want a part of it.

The first group are sold. They are making success look easy. Their business performance metrics have risen. They feel good about themselves. Every metric of staff such as retention and satisfaction is up. They are free to work on their business without the day-to-day demands of providing answers to each question.

The third group that don't want a part of the Asking Leader are fine with me. I watch them work too hard, make too many decisions, answer too many questions. They don't have holidays, their families barely know them, and they are damned unhappy. In one hundred per cent of these cases, the businesses have hit a ceiling. They grow to the level of the CEO and then they stop. They climb to the level that their CEO allows, and then they just stop climbing.

The interesting CEOs are in the middle group. Those who pick up parts. They like the idea and understand the basic concepts.

They learn to listen more clearly and with deeper intent. They practice the listening techniques of being active, repeating and rephrasing the answers and they encourage the contributions.

The middle group are interested in the idea of curiosity. They think about being curious in their conversations and in their general lives when they read, research and participate. The curiosity mindset becomes a part of their nature.

It is the discipline (the self-discipline) where the middle group fall down. Most of my CEOs know they must be disciplined to stay in the Asking Leader mode, but most revert to their natural neural pathway of giving instructions, interrupting, not constructing their series of questions adequately.

For business leaders to create new neural pathways—or replace old behaviours with preferred new behaviours—is a piece of simple psychology. There are four simple steps:

1. **Recognise** the behaviour you want to change. If you want to be disciplined in your conversations and you see that you aren't, that is recognition. Psychologists may call it cognitive behaviour. You can see your behaviour and it isn't what you want.

2. Perform a **physical act** to stop yourself. In James Kerr's book *Legacy*[13] on the All Blacks (2013) he talks of players touching their wrists, looking at the scoreboard. Maria Sharapova does a little jig before each serve to get herself in the correct rhythm to serve to the best of her ability. The physical act is a subtle message to yourself that this is not the leadership behaviour you want to display. The act will make you focus again on the leadership

---

13 Legacy. James Kerr 2013. ISBN 9781472103536

behaviours you do want to display. Psychologists may call this a therapy. Your own in-built therapy.

3. **Change** your behaviour at that point. Go back to asking questions, design a series in your mind, actively listen.

4. **Practice** the new behaviour until it becomes your default behaviour. Your new neural pathway will have been consciously created. The neural pathway to the undesirable behaviour will fade away with practice.

What comes next?

What comes after the Asking Leader for you? If you have created the neural pathway, if you are sufficiently confident in the protocol, what can you do with that? Where will it take you?

Perhaps you can introduce the protocol to your Senior Leadership Team. Perhaps they can introduce it to their managers.

Maybe, a big maybe, you can introduce the protocol to your board of directors. How much would you like another book on how to introduce the Asking Leader into all levels of your business?

Is it possible that you can introduce it to your family?

Take a moment now and think about the impacts of making this change in your personal leadership behaviour. How would it affect your:

1. Senior Leadership Team?
2. their managers?
3. your board of Directors?
4. your family?

How would it affect you? How:

1. you feel about yourself?
2. people will perceive you?
3. effective you can become at achieving your business goals?

The biggest impact of all. You will have friends. You won't have to buy a dog.

Further resources

See www.askingleader.com **for a full list of linked resources.**

Australian Institute of Management, https://www.aim.com.au

Australian Institute of Company Directors, http://aicd. companydirectors.com.au

Australian Rural Leadership Program, https://rural-leaders.org.au,

Stephen R Covey, *7 Habits of Highly Effective People*, Simon & Schuster, New York, 2004

Deloitte, *Culture of Purpose*, 2014, https://www2.deloitte.com/us/en/ pages/about-deloitte/articles/culture-of-purpose.html

Greg Donlan, *The Sales Coach*, https://thesalescoachonline. com/author/greg/, 2018, https://www.youtube.com/ watch?v=yqUDhJvZKSE&t=61s

Robyn Haydon, *Winning Again – A Retention Game Plan for your Most Important Contracts and Customers*, Durban Professionals Press, 2015, http://www.robynhaydon.com

Wiley Miller, *Non Sequitur*, https://www.gocomics.com/nonsequitur/

Lisa Earle McLeod, *Leading with Noble Purpose: How to Create a Tribe of True Believers*, 2016

Richard Paul and Dr Linda Elder, *The Art of Socratic Questioning*, Foundation for Critical Thinking Press, USA, 2007, https:// www.criticalthinking.org/store/get_file.php?inventories_ id=231&inventories_files_id=374

Allan Pease, *'Body language, the power is in the palm of your hands'* TEDxMacquarieUniversity, https://www.bing.com/videos/search?q=allan+pease+you-tube&view=detail&mid=A7496AAE97537C33263FA7496AAE-97537C33263F&FORM=VIRE

Ricardo Semler, *Maverick*, Warner Books, New York, 1993

Simon Sinek, *Start with Why*, Portfolio, New York, 2009

Patrice Thompson, *'A millennial's proposal for a happy multigenerational workplace'*, TED Institute, https://www.ted.com/watch/ted-institute/ted-state-street/patrice-thompson-closing-the-gap-a-millennial-proposal-for-a-happy-multigenerational-workplace

Trial of Socrates, Wikipedia, 2019, https://en.wikipedia.org/wiki/Trial_of_Socrates

Zig Ziglar, https://www.ziglar.com, 2019

Printed in July 2019
by Rotomail Italia S.p.A., Vignate (MI) - Italy